ORIGINS OF OPENING

© 2025 Jason A. Solomon, B.Ed
All rights reserved.

No part of this publication may be reproduced, stored in a retrieval system, or transmitted in any form or by any means – electronic, mechanical, photocopying, recording, or otherwise – without the prior written permission of the publisher, except in the case of brief quotations embodied in critical articles or reviews.

This book is a work of reflective nonfiction and creative spiritual writing. While it draws on universal themes, psychological insight, and symbolic traditions, it is not intended as a substitute for professional mental health, medical, or legal advice.

First Edition
ISBN: 978-1-7638934-8-1
Cover design and interior layout by Aussie Guys Books
Edited and published by Aussie Guys Books

For permissions, speaking engagements, and upcoming releases, visit:
www.aussieguysbooks.com.au

365 Days of SOUL™ is a trademark of Jason A. Solomon.

365 DAYS OF SOUL
VOLUME 2

APRIL
MAY
JUNE

Your Journey Through Time, Shadow, and Spirit

Not all openings come with bloom. Some arrive as breath. As undoing. As readiness.

Jason A. Solomon

Titles in Series
365 Days of SOUL

Seeds of Stillness
Volume 1: January – February – March

Origins of Opening
Volume 2: April – May – June

Unveiling the Unknown
Volume 3: July – August - September

Light in the Layers
Volume 4: October – November - December

Welcome to Volume 2

ORIGINS OF OPENING

Your spiritual companion for the first breath of every day

This is the month of thresholding. Not in the loud,
world-facing way. But in the quiet places where
your inner world has already shifted.
~ And now wants to move ~

How to Use Your Book

Origins of Opening is the second volume in the 365 Days of SOUL series ~ a soulful unfolding of daily entries crafted to help you meet your mornings with tenderness, clarity, and emotional honesty.

This is not a calendar. It is not a checklist.

It is a rhythm. A quiet becoming. A space where your soul has permission to open ~ one breath at a time.

This book offers spiritual presence, emotional steadiness, and soulful encouragement ~ all gently woven into the first moments of your day.

For each day:

Let this book greet you before the world does. Before notifications. Before obligation. Even before your feet touch the floor.

This is your morning companion ~ a grounding hand for the you who is still tender with sleep, still open to the day's direction.

For each entry, you'll receive:

- A Soul Reflection or Narrative Moment ~ to meet the emotional energy of the day
- The Daily Archetype ~ the part of your psyche or spirit emerging today
- Sacred Wisdom ~ drawn from nature, philosophy, numerology, and symbolism

- A **Reflection Prompts:** ~ to invite quiet self-inquiry
- A Gentle Practice or Embodiment Tool ~ to integrate soul into your day

Read. Breathe. Soften. Begin Again.

Let the words speak to the part of you that's ready to grow.

You don't need to finish every page. Sometimes one line is enough.

.

Seasonal Awareness:: April - June

Whether you're in the Northern Hemisphere, awakening into spring, or the Southern Hemisphere, deepening into autumn, this book honors both the visible and invisible transitions that come with this season.

Spring invites movement. Autumn invites reflection. Both ask the same thing:

"What is ready to open now?"

Each daily entry reflects this sacred dialogue ~ between your inner growth and the rhythm of the earth.

You'll find moments of clarity, courage, boundary-setting, emotion, and emerging purpose.

There is no right way to move forward ~ only your way.

Why Opening is Good?

Because before we grow, we must loosen. Before we shine, we must stretch. Before we move, we must feel what is true.

This season is not about speed. It is about intention ~ about letting the soul bloom at its own pace.

Let these pages open gently, like petals in your hands.

Let your thoughts find stillness before direction.

Let your inner life come alive before your outer life begins.

"You do not need to force your growth, you only need to make space for it."

Contents

April 1 - The Day of Hidden Blooming 18

April 2 – The Day of Emotional Honesty 21

April 3 – The Day of Inner Courage 24

April 4 – The Day of Gentle Boundaries 27

April 5 – The Day of Soul Rhythm 30

April 6 – The Day of Soul Witnessing 33

April 7 – The Day of Anchored Trust 36

April 8 – The Day of Embodied Wisdom 39

April 9 – The Day of Soft Resilience 42

April 10 – The Day of Soul Alignment 45

April 11 – The Day of Sacred Curiosity 48

April 12 – The Day of Self-Compassion 51

April 13 – The Day of Purposeful Presence 54

April 14 – The Day of Emotional Courage 57

April 15 – The Day of Restful Power 60

April 16 – The Day of Soul Listening 63

April 17 – The Day of Devoted Choice 66

April 18 – The Day of Inner Renewal 69

April 19 – The Day of Subtle Expansion 72

April 20 – The Day of Grounded Becoming 75

April 21 – The Day of Sacred Self-Belief 78

April 22 – The Day of Earth-Rooted Wisdom 81

April 23 – The Day of Sacred Boundaries 84

April 24 – The Day of Soul Recognition 87

April 25 – The Day of Quiet Devotion 90
April 26 – The Day of Unshakable Calm 93
April 27 – The Day of Authentic Expression 96
April 28 – The Day of Soulful Connection 99
April 29 – The Day of Embodied Grace 102
April 30 – The Day of Integration 105
April Reflection 108
May 1 – The Day of Inner Blooming 112
May 2 – The Day of Soulful Invitation 115
May 3 – The Day of Emotional Undress 118
May 4 – The Day of Erotic Presence 121
May 5 – The Day of Vulnerable Union 124
May 6 – The Day of Shared Breath 127
May 7 – The Day of Soulful Surrender 130
May 8 – The Day of Inner Devotion 134
May 9 – The Day of Healing Desire 137
May 10 – The Day of Sacred Touch 141
May 11 – The Day of Union and Release 145
May 12 – The Day of Intimate Trust 148
May 13 – The Day of Sensual Receiving 152
May 14 – The Day of Soul-Made Sex 156
May 15 – The Day of Loving Integration 160
May 16 – The Day of Emotional Communion 164
May 17 – The Day of Sacred Slowness 168
May 18 – The Day of Tender Power 171
May 19 – The Day of Sacred Boundaries in Love 175

May 20 – The Day of Reverent Closeness 179

May 21 – The Day of Magnetic Honesty 183

May 22 – The Day of Sensory Union 186

May 23 – The Day of Erotic Self-Trust......................................190

May 24 – The Day of Deep Listening in Love 193

May 25 – The Day of Sacred Sensation....................................197

May 26 – The Day of Embodied Truth.....................................200

May 27 – The Day of Mutual Awakening 203

May 28 – The Day of Sensual Grace..207

May 29 – The Day of Sacred Memory......................................210

May 30 – The Day of Erotic Stillness..213

May 31 – The Day of Intimate Renewal..................................216

May Reflection...220

June 1 – The Day of Body Wisdom..226

June 2 – The Day of Erotic Simplicity......................................230

June 3 – The Day of Loving Clarity...234

June 4 – The Day of Rooted Sensuality....................................238

June 5 – The Day of Wild Permission 242

June 6 – The Day of Devotional Desire....................................246

June 7 – The Day of Soulful Submission 250

June 8 – The Day of Grounded Passion 254

June 9 – The Day of Unfiltered Intimacy.................................258

June 10 – The Day of Sensual Presence 262

June 11 – The Day of Embodied Honesty 266

June 12 – The Day of Sacred Reconnection...........................270

June 13 – The Day of Vulnerable Fire......................................275

June 14 – The Day of Erotic Equilibrium 280
June 15 – The Day of Inner Union 284
June 16 – The Day of Soulful Boundaries 288
June 17 – The Day of Erotic Truth 292
June 18 – The Day of Sacred Mirrors 297
June 19 – The Day of Intimate Integrity 302
June 20 – The Day of Soulful Reciprocity 307
June 21 – The Day of Seasonal Turning 311
June 22 – The Day of Devotional Presence 315
June 23 – The Day of Heart-Safe Expression 319
June 24 – The Day of Emotional Sanctuary 323
June 25 – The Day of Tender Courage 327
June 26 – The Day of Shared Healing 333
June 27 – The Day of Sensory Awakening 337
June 28 – The Day of Inner Nourishment 341
June 29 – The Day of Quiet Devotion 345
June 30 – The Day of Inner Celebration 349
June Reflection 354
Notes 359
Your Journey Deepens 362

*Welcome to this season of becoming.
Welcome ~ again ~ to yourself.*

April 1 - The Day of Hidden Blooming

A story of unseen growth, quiet courage, and the unfolding that begins before anyone can see it

There once was a soul who thought blooming had to be visible.

They believed transformation needed to be shared. That growth should be impressive. That opening meant being seen ~ clearly, brightly, out loud.

But they were tired. Not from effort, but from expectation ~ the kind that turns natural growth into performance.

Then, one morning ~ as light shifted in the Northern Hemisphere toward spring or softened in the Southern Hemisphere into early autumn ~ the soul felt something stir.

It wasn't big. It wasn't loud. It was a breath.

Something had changed inside them ~ even if no one else could tell.

"Maybe this is enough," the soul thought. "Maybe I don't need to bloom in public."

They placed a hand over their chest and exhaled. And in that breath… something opened.

April 1 carries the energy of 1, the number of beginnings, identity, and initiation. But this is not the bold start of January 1 ~ this is a quieter beginning. A blooming from *beneath*.

Today, you are not being asked to make anything known. You are simply invited to notice: What is beginning inside me… even if no one else sees it?

The archetype of the day is The Quiet Blossom ~ the soul that doesn't rush its opening or demand to be witnessed.

The one that allows growth to be *felt first* before being shown.

This day honors the hidden effort, the subtle shift, the sacred *becoming* that occurs out of sight.

Today's Symbols::

- A bud held closed by morning dew, still gathering strength
- Rose quartz, for self-compassion and unforced openness
- The Four of Pentacles, holding what is precious ~ not out of fear, but care
- A rabbit, still in the grass, heart racing, sensing its own readiness

Reflective Prompts: Where in my life am I opening inwardly ~ even if it's not visible yet?

- What does it feel like to grow without proving?
- Can I trust the part of me that is unfolding privately?

Integration Practice: The Unseen Garden

Choose a small object ~ a stone, leaf, shell, or crystal. Keep it with you or place it by your bed.

Each morning this week, hold it in your palm and whisper:

"I am blooming in ways no one can see."

Let it become a quiet altar to your becoming ~ private, sacred, real.

You don't need validation for growth to be true.

Closing Mantra for the Today ~

"I honor what is opening in me ~ even if no one else sees it. My quiet blooming is enough."

April 2 – The Day of Emotional Honesty

A story of inner truth, courageous softness, and the healing that happens when you stop hiding what you really feel

There once was a soul who learned early that feelings were fragile things.

Too much sadness made others uncomfortable. Too much anger made them unlikable. Too much joy, even ~ and they risked being called "too much."

So they became careful. Contained. Curated.

They smiled through heartbreak. Shrugged through the disappointment. Nodded through the confusion.

But one morning ~ as blossoms appeared in the North or leaves turned amber in the South ~ something inside the soul became too tender to keep wrapped.

A single sentence rose in their chest:

"I don't want to pretend anymore."

Not for attention. Not for drama. But because honesty… felt like oxygen.

April 2 carries the energy of 2, the number of emotional attunement, truth in relationship, and sacred mirroring.

This is a day to stop managing how others feel about you ~ and start honoring how *you* feel within you.

It's not about full disclosure. It's about *integrity*. Not broadcasting emotion ~ but allowing it.

The archetype of the day is The Honest Heart ~ the part of you that speaks not to be loud, but to be *real*.

This part doesn't need permission to feel. It needs acceptance ~ and a safe place to land.

Today's Symbols::

- A fogged-up mirror slowly clearing, revealing emotion underneath
- Aquamarine, for truth-telling and emotional equilibrium
- The Page of Cups, innocence in feeling, willingness to express
- A dove, cooing softly ~ not to be heard, but because it's how it breathes

Reflection Prompts:

- What emotion have I been suppressing for the sake of others' comfort?

- What part of me needs to be spoken aloud ~ even if only to myself?
- Where in my body do I feel truth rising? And what happens when I allow it to move?

Integration Practice: One Truth Sentence

At some point today, write or speak one emotionally honest sentence ~ no more, no less.

It could be:

- "I feel overwhelmed, and I need gentleness today."
- "I'm excited, even if I'm scared to admit it."
- "I miss something I can't name."
- "I'm angry about what I accepted for too long."

Whisper it to yourself. Speak it to a page. Or share it, safely, with someone you trust.

This is not confession. It's *connection*.

Closing Mantra for the Today ~ ~

"My truth is worthy of breath. My emotions are sacred messengers. I speak with softness and courage."

April 3 – The Day of Inner Courage

A story of quiet bravery, sacred discomfort, and the kind of courage that doesn't roar ~ it just keeps going

There once was a soul who thought courage had to be dramatic.

They believed it came in bold moves and big declarations ~ in climbing mountains, quitting jobs, or walking away with fierce resolve.

But most days didn't feel like that.

Most days, courage looked smaller: Getting out of bed when the world felt heavy. Speaking up in a room where they once stayed quiet. Letting themselves hope… even after being hurt.

One day ~ as winds shifted with early spring in the North, or deepened into dusk in the South ~ the soul realized:

"Maybe courage isn't what I do for show. Maybe it's what I do for *me*."

And suddenly, everything brave they had done quietly… counted.

April 3 carries the energy of 3, a number of movement, voice, and willpower. But in this unfolding season, that power is not loud ~ it's grounded in truth.

This is a day to honor the inner courage that fuels your healing, your boundaries, your soft growth.

Not the leaps.

But the steps.

The archetype of the day is The Quiet Lion ~ the part of you that doesn't need applause, but still shows up. The part that keeps choosing growth even when it's uncomfortable.

Today's Symbols::

- A small stone on a mountain path, unnoticed but holding everything in place
- Carnelian, for motivation, courage, and creative energy
- The Strength card, not forceful ~ but gentle, determined, inwardly anchored
- A badger, steady and low to the ground, fierce when necessary, deeply loyal to its own rhythm

Reflection Prompts:

- What has taken courage from me recently ~ even if no one else noticed?
- Where am I being quietly brave in my daily life?

- What would it look like to acknowledge that courage… without minimizing it?

Integration Practice: Name Your Courage

Write a short list of 3 courageous things you've done in the past month.

They don't need to look big. They need to feel true.

Examples:

- "I rested when I was tired ~ even when it made me feel guilty."
- "I shared my real opinion instead of agreeing automatically."
- "I kept showing up for myself even when it felt hard."

Circle the one that cost the most emotional energy. Whisper to yourself:

"That counts. That was brave."

Closing Mantra for the Today ~

"My courage does not need to be seen to be real. I honor the bravery of my becoming."

April 4 – The Day of Gentle Boundaries

A story of soft protection, self-respect, and learning that love doesn't mean saying yes to everything

There once was a soul who wanted to be kind.

They said yes often. Made space for others. Gave more than they had.

They believed kindness meant availability ~ that love meant sacrifice, that being a "good person" meant having no edges.

But over time, they grew tired.

Not the kind of tired that rest could fix ~ but the kind that comes from leaking energy… drop by drop… day after day.

Then one morning ~ in the fresh breath of Northern spring or the golden hush of Southern autumn ~ they paused.

They put a hand on their heart and asked:

"What if boundaries aren't rejection… but a way of remembering who I am?"

And in that moment, they said a quiet no. It was soft. It was real. It was *holy*.

April 4 holds the double resonance of 4 ~ structure, foundation, and sustainable care.

This is a day to tend your edges with kindness. To recognize that gentle boundaries don't keep people out ~ they keep *you* in.

Not a wall. Not a weapon. A signal: *This is where my peace lives.*

The archetype of the day is The Loving Guardian ~ the self who protects without punishing, who knows that saying "no" can be the most intimate act of self-trust.

Today's Symbols::

- A circle drawn in soft sand, complete but impermanent
- Pink opal, for emotional clarity and heart-centered protection
- The Queen of Swords, wise, discerning, still open
- A turtle, not hiding ~ but choosing when to emerge

Reflection Prompts:

- Where in my life am I giving out of habit ~ not from wholeness?
- What "yes" have I said recently that needs to become a "no"?
- What might it feel like to disappoint someone gently… in order to honor myself honestly?

Integration Practice: Rewriting the "No" Narrative

Finish the sentence:

"When I set a boundary, it means…"

Then rewrite it with truth, not guilt.

Example:

- Old story: "When I set a boundary, it means I'm pushing people away."
- True story: "When I set a boundary, it means I'm choosing what supports my energy and connection."

Repeat it aloud ~ like a vow.

You are allowed to be whole and protected.

Closing Mantra for the Today ~

"My boundaries are not barriers. They are bridges to deeper self-respect."

April 5 – The Day of Soul Rhythm

A story of inner timing, sacred pacing, and learning to move at the speed of your spirit ~ not the speed of the world

There once was a soul who could never quite keep up.

They tried. They copied the routines of others. Woke up early, hustled hard, made lists.

But something always felt off. Too fast. Too much. Too... *not them*.

They began to believe something was wrong with them ~ that maybe they were lazy, unmotivated, or slow.

Until one day ~ as life began stirring in the Northern spring, or softening into reflection in the Southern autumn ~ the soul stopped following the clock.

They listened to their own breath. To their own rise and fall. To their own *rhythm*.

And they realized...

"My pace is not a problem. It is a language."

April 5 carries the energy of 5, the number of movement, change, and personal flow. But today's movement isn't hurried ~ it's *attuned*.

This is a day to tune in to your soul's rhythm ~ to ask not "what should I do?" but "how am I moving right now?"

Are you in a season of planting? Pausing? Pulsing? Let that answer shape your actions ~ not anyone else's pace.

The archetype of the day is The Inner Dancer ~ the part of you that knows when to leap and when to rest. The part that finds freedom not in intensity, but in alignment.

Today's Symbols::

- A drumbeat echoing in a quiet forest, calling inward
- Labradorite, for intuitive flow and energetic awareness
- The Two of Pentacles, harmonizing movement, balancing life's motion
- A hummingbird, moving swiftly ~ but always pausing to receive

Reflection Prompts:

- What is the current rhythm of my life ~ and does it match my inner pace?
- Where am I rushing because I think I "should"?
- What does it feel like when I move in sync with my body, spirit, and emotions?

Integration Practice: The Rhythm Check-In

Throughout today, pause at three points ~ morning, midday, evening ~ and ask:

"Am I moving in my true rhythm right now?"

If the answer is no, take a single breath to reset. Step away. Slow down. Speed up. Rest. Whatever honors your internal pulse.

Let this question become your guide for the next week. Not to restrict you ~ but to *free* you.

Closing Mantra for the Today ~

"I move at the pace of my becoming. My rhythm is sacred. My pace is wise."

April 6 ~ The Day of Soul Witnessing

A story of presence without judgment, sacred attention, and the quiet power of simply being with what is

There once was a soul who always tried to fix.

They offered advice quickly. They interrupted with encouragement. They listened with the intent to *help* ~ not to hear.

But beneath it all, they longed for someone to do for them what they so often did for others:

To *stay*. To *see*. To hold space ~ without solving.

One afternoon ~ in the tender greening of the Northern spring, or the golden hush of the Southern fall ~ the soul sat beneath a tree and heard nothing but wind.

They didn't reach for distraction. Didn't reach for a reason.

They just *watched*. They *witnessed*.

And in that moment, something deep within them whispered:

"This is what I've needed. And this is what I can offer ~ to others and myself."

April 6 carries the energy of 6, the number of harmony, relational care, and presence. But presence isn't just being nearby ~ it is deep noticing without interference.

Today invites you to become a soul witness ~ someone who doesn't rush to react, but chooses to *see clearly and stay connected.*

This applies to how you show up for others... and how you show up for *yourself.*

The archetype of the day is The Soul Witness ~ the quiet observer who holds space with grace, who knows that sometimes healing doesn't come from being fixed... but from being *fully seen.*

Today's Symbols::

- A still lake reflecting the sky, undisturbed, complete
- Moonstone, for intuitive witnessing and gentle emotional holding
- The High Priestess, she who sees inwardly and waits without forcing
- An owl, perched quietly in the trees ~ watching, knowing, not intervening

Reflection Prompts:

- Where in my life am I trying to fix something that simply wants to be witnessed?

- How can I hold space for my emotions without changing or justifying them?
- Who in my life needs presence more than advice ~ and can I offer that today?

Integration Practice: The 5-Minute Witness

Set a timer for 5 minutes. Sit silently with yourself. No music. No phone. No task.

Simply notice:

- What's rising in your body
- What thoughts cycle through
- What feelings are present beneath the noise

You're not here to solve anything. You're here to stay present.

At the end, whisper:

"I see you. I am here."

Say it as both a giver and a receiver.

Closing Mantra for the Today ~

"I do not need to fix. I do not need to rush. I witness with love. I stay with truth."

April 7 – The Day of Anchored Trust

A story of steady faith, grounded hope, and learning to trust what can't yet be seen

There once was a soul who needed certainty.

They craved signs. Proof. Guarantees. A plan with no room for surprises.

They'd been disappointed before ~ so now, they clung to control like a lifeline.

But control is heavy. And fear? Even heavier.

One grey and golden morning ~ as early blossoms trembled in the North, or dry leaves whispered across the Southern soil ~ the soul paused.

They didn't have answers. Only a heartbeat. A breath. A longing to *let go*.

So they did. Not completely. Not forever. But just enough to say:

"I don't know what's next… but I don't have to collapse while I wait for it."

And in that breath, they felt something steady ~ not above them, but *within*.

April 7 carries the energy of 7, a number of trust, spiritual alignment, and deeper knowing. But today is not about blind faith ~ it's about *anchored trust*.

The kind you build quietly. The kind that doesn't disappear in the unknown.

This is a day to root into something deeper than certainty ~ to find steadiness in the absence of clear outcomes.

The archetype of the day is The Grounded Believer ~ the soul who walks forward not because they see the whole path, but because they trust their own footing.

Today's Symbols::

- A stone half-buried in rich earth, unmoved by wind or water
- Hematite, for grounding, clarity, and energetic anchoring
- The Star card, hope born from truth, not illusion
- A whale deep underwater, singing a song no one hears ~ but still true

Reflection Prompts:

- What am I waiting to feel "ready" for ~ and what if trust is the readiness?
- Where in my life do I crave control ~ and what truth lies beneath that craving?

— How can I root into faith that doesn't erase fear, but steadies me through it?

Integration Practice: Create a Trust Tether

Write down one sentence you want to anchor into ~ a sentence that feels like a truth, even if it's still becoming real.

Examples:

- "I can handle uncertainty one breath at a time."
- "Something in me already knows the way."
- "I don't need to see it all to take the next step."

Write it on a card. Carry it today. Hold it like a stone in your palm when the wind of doubt rises.

This is your tether ~ not to outcomes, but to *yourself*.

Closing Mantra for the Today ~

"I trust not because I know ~ but because I am anchored in who I am."

April 8 – The Day of Embodied Wisdom

A story of lived truth, cellular knowing, and the sacred intelligence of the body

There once was a soul who lived in their head.

They loved knowledge. Collected quotes. Highlighted books. Listened to teachers, mentors, and podcasts with eager devotion.

But for all the understanding they had ~ they still felt disconnected. Stuck. Unfulfilled.

Because something essential was missing.

One morning ~ under lengthening skies in the North, or the descending hush of early Southern autumn ~ they stopped searching *out there*.

They took a breath. Placed both hands on their belly. And listened.

Not to a thought. But to a pulse. A hum. A truth that didn't need to be said aloud.

"You've always known," their body whispered. "Now… live it."

April 8 carries the energy of 8, the number of integration, power, and embodied alignment. Today invites you to *stop reading your wisdom* and start living it.

This is not a day to overexplain, overprocess, or overplan. It's a day to feel what's already true ~ and let that lead you.

The archetype of the day is The Embodied Sage ~ the one who doesn't preach or strive, but simply walks as wisdom. Whose life becomes the teaching.

Today's Symbols::

- A hand pressed to the heart, still and strong
- Amethyst, for spiritual clarity and somatic truth
- The Hierophant, not as an external authority, but as the inner guide made real
- A mountain goat, grounded, deliberate, wise in its footing

Reflection Prompts:

- What truth do I keep relearning intellectually ~ but haven't yet embodied?
- Where do I feel my intuition in my body ~ and what does it ask of me?
- What if I let my actions become my wisdom ~ even in small, quiet ways?

Integration Practice: Head to Heart to Body

Try this simple centering ritual:

- Touch your forehead and name one insight you've been holding.

Ex: "I know I need rest."

- Touch your heart and feel into what it means emotionally.

"I feel tired, stretched, overextended."

- Touch your lower belly and choose one way to honor that in your day.

"Today, I will cancel one task to make space."

Let the wisdom move *through* you ~ not just *to* you.

Closing Mantra for the Today ~

"I no longer seek to know ~ I seek to live what I already know."

April 9 – The Day of Soft Resilience

A story of quiet strength, flexible endurance, and the kind of resilience that bends without breaking

There once was a soul who misunderstood resilience.

They thought it meant pushing through. Holding it together. Saying "I'm fine" even when their heart was breaking.

They wore strength like armor ~ tight, polished, unyielding.

But over time, the weight became too much. Not because they were weak ~ but because they were *ready* to stop pretending.

One day ~ as young buds reached for light in the North, or leaves loosened their grip in the South ~ the soul watched a blade of grass bend in the wind.

It didn't snap. It didn't fight. It *swayed*. And when the wind passed, it stood again.

"That," the soul whispered, "is what I want to be."

Not invincible. Just real ~ and rooted.

April 9 carries the energy of 9, the number of wisdom, maturity, and soul integration. Today is not about toughness ~ it's about *resilient softness.*

This is the day to honor how you've endured ~ not by force, but by *flexibility*. Not by denying your pain, but by staying open through it.

The archetype of the day is The Gentle Survivor ~ the one who learns that resilience doesn't harden, it *softens with strength.*

Today's Symbols::

- A willow branch, bending in wind, never breaking
- Moss agate, for grounding through softness and steady inner healing
- The Nine of Wands, battle-worn but still standing ~ not to fight, but to *witness*
- A sea lion, resting on a rock between waves ~ strong and soft at once

Reflection Prompts:

- Where in my life have I confused numbness with resilience?
- What would soft strength look like for me today?
- What part of me is asking to be resilient in a new way ~ one that includes rest, honesty, and tenderness?

Integration Practice: The Resilience Redefinition

Write down your old definition of resilience. Be honest.

"Resilience means…" (e.g. "never stopping," "never crying," "always coping")

Now, write a new definition that reflects what your soul actually needs:

"Resilience now means…" (e.g. "knowing when to pause," "feeling and moving forward," "asking for help without shame")

Keep this visible. Let it guide your recovery, not just your strength.

Closing Mantra for the Today ~

"I do not need to harden to survive. My softness is my strength. I bend. I heal. I rise."

April 10 – The Day of Soul Alignment

A story of internal harmony, quiet clarity, and choosing the path that matches who you truly are

There once was a soul who lived divided.

They said one thing, felt another. Agreed to things their body resisted. Chased what looked "right" instead of what felt *true*.

It wasn't dishonesty ~ it was survival. They wanted to be liked. Needed. Belonging. But over time, the cost became clear.

One cool morning ~ as spring rains nourished the North, or long shadows stretched across Southern soil ~ the soul came to a fork in the path.

One way was familiar. Predictable. Approved of.

The other? Quieter. Less certain. But deeply… *right*.

They didn't rush. They didn't decide for applause.

They chose the way that felt like home ~ inside their chest.

"This," the soul whispered, "is what it means to live in alignment."

April 10 carries the energy of 1 (1 + 0), the number of beginning again ~ but this time from the *inside out*.

Today invites you to notice the places where your words, choices, and values are asking to meet each other again ~ not for perfection, but for *peace*.

The archetype of the day is The Aligned Seeker ~ the soul that stops performing and starts *practicing* truth. Whose path may be unconventional, but always feels honest.

Today's Symbols::

- A compass resting on bare soil, pointing not north ~ but inward
- Amazonite, for honest communication and energetic alignment
- The Justice card, not for judgment, but for soul-level harmony
- A heron, walking slowly in shallow water ~ each step precise, intuitive, real

Reflection Prompts:

- Where in my life am I out of alignment ~ saying yes when I mean no, or staying still when I long to move?
- What truth am I ready to return to ~ even if it's uncomfortable?

- How would my choices shift if I trusted my inner compass more than others' approval?

Integration Practice: Alignment Audit

Draw three circles side by side.

Label them:

- What I do
- What I say I value
- What I feel in my body

Take 5 minutes to jot down a few notes in each. Then ask yourself:

Where do these match? Where do they misalign?

You don't need to fix it all today. But awareness is the first step toward a life that feels *whole*.

Closing Mantra for the Today ~

"I choose the path that aligns with my soul. Even quietly. Even slowly. Even if only I understand it."

April 11 – The Day of Sacred Curiosity

A story of wonder, deeper questioning, and the soul's invitation to explore without needing to arrive

There once was a soul who was tired of answers.

They had gathered facts, formed opinions, built neat explanations around things they didn't fully feel.

But the more answers they had, the less alive they felt.

Certainty had become a cage.

Then one morning ~ as the Northern world bloomed into new color or the Southern world exhaled into gold ~ the soul asked a question they didn't expect:

"What if not knowing is where I meet the divine?"

And in that space of not knowing ~ something softened. Something opened.

The soul wasn't lost. It was just finally *free* to wonder again.

April 11 carries the energy of 2 (1 + 1), the number of duality, dialogue, and relational discovery.

Today's wisdom lives not in answers, but in the willingness to ask questions that make you more *aware* ~ not more certain. This is a day to hold your life like a riddle ~ not a riddle to be solved, but *lived*.

The archetype of the day is The Curious Mystic ~ the part of you that kneels beside mystery and listens, not for facts, but for *resonance*.

Today's Symbols::

- A key that fits no known lock, carried just in case
- Iolite, the stone of inner vision and intuitive exploration
- The Page of Swords, open, alert, and full of wonder
- A fox, alert in the shadows, investigating with delight ~ not fear

Reflection Prompts:

- What question has been quietly circling my life ~ one I've avoided or minimized?
- Where might wonder bring more clarity than control?
- What if the unknown isn't my enemy ~ but my next threshold?

Integration Practice: The Living Question

Instead of journaling answers today, write a question that you will *carry* for the next week.

Start it with:

"What might shift if I…" "Why do I keep returning to…" "What is my soul inviting me to see in this?"

Place it somewhere you'll see each morning. Don't try to answer it. Let it open you ~ again and again.

Closing Mantra for the Today ~

"I honor what I do not yet know. Curiosity is my courage. Mystery is not a problem ~ it is a portal."

April 12 – The Day of Self-Compassion

A story of inner gentleness, radical permission, and learning to love yourself in the moment you're in ~ not the one you're trying to reach

There once was a soul who could extend kindness to everyone but themselves.

They forgave others quickly. Held space for mistakes. Offered softness, understanding, grace.

But when it came to their own missteps ~ the bar was higher. The voice was harsher. The compassion vanished.

Until one afternoon ~ beneath new blossoms in the North, or the soft rust of falling leaves in the South ~ they sat down, weary from their own expectations.

They wrapped a blanket around their shoulders. Closed their eyes. And whispered the words they had longed to hear:

"I forgive you. I love you. You don't have to be perfect to be worthy of peace."

They didn't transform in that moment. They simply became *real*.

April 12 carries the energy of 3 (1 + 2), the number of expression, self-awareness, and healing communication. Today is not about performance or proving ~ it's about *presence with the parts of yourself you often neglect.*

This is a day to meet yourself where you are ~ not after the next achievement or improvement, but *now*.

The archetype of the day is The Inner Healer ~ the self who knows how to soothe rather than push, who replaces perfectionism with presence, and who offers love not *after* the hard moment, but *during* it.

Today's Symbols::

- A worn quilt draped over open shoulders, stitched with many colors
- Rhodochrosite, for emotional healing, forgiveness, and tender self-acceptance
- The Temperance card, healing through balance, patience, and kindness
- A koala, resting calmly in its tree ~ peaceful without striving

Reflection Prompts:

- Where have I been pushing myself instead of caring for myself?
- What part of me needs kindness today ~ not correction?

— How might my life feel different if I treated myself with the softness I give to others?

Integration Practice: The Compassion Mirror

Stand or sit in front of a mirror.

Look gently into your eyes.

Say aloud (even if it feels awkward):

"You've tried so hard. I see that. You are allowed to be tired. You are allowed to be loved. You are already enough."

Even once is enough. Even a whisper counts.

This is how self-compassion takes root ~ word by word, breath by breath.

Closing Mantra for the Today ~

"I release the pressure to be better before I'm worthy. I meet myself with love ~ here, now, as I am."

April 13 – The Day of Purposeful Presence

A story of grounded attention, meaningful moments, and the quiet power of choosing to be fully here

There once was a soul who always felt one step ahead or one step behind.

They rushed through mornings thinking of the afternoon. They replayed yesterday while missing today. Their body was present, but their mind… wandered.

One day ~ beneath early cherry blossoms in the North, or under the muted hush of turning trees in the South ~ the soul paused in the middle of doing something ordinary.

A cup of tea. The sound of wind. The way the light hit the floor.

And for the first time in a long time, they noticed: they were *here*.

Nothing profound happened. But everything *real* did.

"Maybe presence doesn't need to be perfect," the soul whispered. "Maybe it just needs to be *chosen*."

April 13 carries the energy of 4 (1 + 3), the number of foundation, daily rhythm, and embodied mindfulness. Today reminds us that life doesn't happen in the big moments we wait for ~ it happens in the quiet ones we often miss.

This is a day to return to the moment you're in ~ not with pressure, but with purpose.

The archetype of the day is The Present Walker ~ the soul who steps gently into now, not to escape the past or fix the future, but to experience what is true *right here*.

Today's Symbols::

- A bare foot pressing into soft earth, steady and real
- Smoky quartz, for grounded clarity and embodied presence
- The Knight of Pentacles, moving slowly with care and intention
- A deer, alert and aware, attuned to the details of its world

Reflection Prompts:

- What part of my day today can I give my full attention to ~ without multitasking or rushing?
- What does it feel like when I am truly present with myself ~ body, mind, and breath?
- Where might I be missing the sacred because I'm waiting for the spectacular?

Integration Practice: The "One Thing" Ritual

Choose one small activity today ~ brushing your teeth, drinking water, making the bed.

Do it slowly. Do it with full attention. Do it without distraction ~ no phone, no music, no multitasking.

Let it be a mini ceremony of now.

You don't need more time. You need more presence.

Closing Mantra for the Today ~

"I don't need to be anywhere else to be whole. I choose this moment. I choose to be here."

April 14 – The Day of Emotional Courage

A story of vulnerability, brave expression, and the power that rises when you speak your heart ~ even if your voice shakes

There once was a soul who feared being too much.

Too intense. Too sensitive. Too emotional.

So they learned to hold things in ~ carefully, quietly. They smiled when they were hurting. Agreed when they wanted to scream. They became fluent in hiding.

But emotions have gravity. And truth eventually finds a voice.

One twilight ~ beneath a rain-washed sky in the North, or in the quiet glow of autumn's descent in the South ~ the soul stood in front of someone they loved and finally spoke what they had never said:

"This is how I really feel."

It wasn't perfect. It wasn't polished. But it was *honest*.

And that made it holy.

April 14 carries the energy of 5 (1 + 4), a number of freedom, self-expression, and inner truth. Today is not about emotional drama ~ it is about emotional courage: the willingness to be *seen in your feeling* without shame.

This is a day to let go of emotional suppression and invite truth forward ~ gently, bravely, and with self-respect.

The archetype of the day is The Heart-Speaker ~ the self who knows that emotional expression isn't weakness; it's *alchemy*.

Today's Symbols::

- A river rising after rain, flowing fully and freely
- Blue calcite, for soothing expression and emotional openness
- The King of Cups, emotionally mature, grounded in feeling without overwhelm
- A wolf, howling not to threaten ~ but to connect

Reflection Prompts:

- What emotion have I been holding back ~ and what has it cost me?
- What would emotional honesty look like today ~ with myself or someone else?
- Can I let myself be seen, not to be understood ~ but to be real?

Integration Practice: The One-Feeling Truth

Set aside 10 quiet minutes.

Ask yourself:

What feeling have I been avoiding or pushing down?

Name it. Feel where it lives in your body.

Now complete this sentence (in writing or aloud):

"The truth is, I feel _____ about _____."

Let the sentence be imperfect. Let it be true. You don't have to act on it. But letting it *exist* is a sacred act.

Closing Mantra for the Today ~

"My emotions are not too much. My truth is worthy of breath. I speak, not to be fixed ~ but to be free."

April 15 – The Day of Restful Power

A story of strength reclaimed in stillness, the quiet force of surrender, and learning that rest is not weakness ~ it's wisdom

There once was a soul who believed power came only through doing.

They hustled. They produced. They held it all together.

Rest, to them, felt dangerous. If they stopped, things might fall apart. If they paused, someone else might take their place.

But inside, the exhaustion grew louder than the voice of ambition.

One early morning ~ beneath the cloud-softened light of spring in the North, or under the wind-stilled trees of the Southern fall ~ the soul sat on the edge of their bed and didn't move.

They didn't reach for their phone. They didn't plan the day. They just… breathed.

And in that space of non-doing, they realized:

"I am still powerful ~ even in pause. Especially in pause."

April 15 carries the energy of 6 (1 + 5), a number of integration, balance, and care of the whole self. Today is not about striving ~ it's about *redefining strength*.

Rest is not what happens when you've run out of energy. Rest is what *protects* your energy.

This is a day to honor your need for pause, slowness, and inner recalibration ~ without apology.

The archetype of the day is The Rested Warrior ~ the soul who understands that action without recovery is erosion… and that power without rest is *unsustainable*.

Today's Symbols::

- A stone circle surrounded by soft moss, still and centered
- Lepidolite, for nervous system restoration and emotional reset
- The Four of Swords, sacred stillness after movement ~ reflection before reengagement
- A bear, curled in hibernation ~ not idle, but healing

Reflection Prompts:

- What do I believe about rest ~ and who taught me that?
- Where in my life am I using "busyness" to avoid listening inward?

— What would it feel like to rest without guilt ~ as a radical return to myself?

Integration Practice: The Sacred 20 Minutes

Today, schedule a 20-minute block of intentional rest. Not sleep. Not distraction. Just *being*.

Lie down. Sit by a window. Walk slowly. No multitasking. No fixing.

Before you begin, whisper:

"I am allowed to stop. I am still whole when I rest."

Let these 20 minutes remind your body that your worth is not earned through exhaustion.

Closing Mantra for the Today ~

"I honor the wisdom in stillness. Rest is not my retreat ~ it is my return."

April 16 – The Day of Soul Listening

A story of deep attunement, quiet revelation, and the sacred truth that emerges when we learn to truly hear ourselves

There once was a soul who filled every silence.

They played music while they cooked. Scrolled between tasks. Filled their calendar so there would be no empty space to face.

Silence made them nervous. Stillness felt like something was missing.

But one day ~ while walking through early blooming fields in the North, or watching leaves gather in the South's soft dusk ~ the soul forgot to bring their distractions.

There was no sound. No voice. Just the wind, the breath, and the *presence* of everything they'd been avoiding.

And in that rare quiet, something spoke:

"I've been here, all along. You just haven't heard me."

It wasn't a voice of fear. It was the voice of *truth* ~ gentle, waiting, whole.

April 16 carries the energy of 7 (1 + 6), the number of deep insight, spiritual sensitivity, and intuitive intelligence. Today invites you to practice soul listening ~ the kind that doesn't just hear noise, but *receives meaning*.

This is not about answers. It's about *attunement*. Not the kind you do with your ears ~ but with your *whole being*.

The archetype of the day is The Soul Listener ~ the part of you who can hear the unspoken, who holds space for nuance, and who understands that truth often arrives in a whisper, not a shout.

Today's Symbols::

- A hollow tree filled with echoes, waiting
- Celestite, for clear connection to the soul's voice and gentle self-trust
- The High Priestess, she who waits, receives, and knows without needing to explain
- A white owl, watching in silence, hearing the world beneath the world

Reflection Prompts:

- When was the last time I truly listened ~ without rushing to respond or fix?
- What parts of me have been speaking through tension, dreams, or silence?

— What wisdom might rise if I gave myself the gift of true attention today?

Integration Practice: The 3-Minute Listening Room

Find a quiet space. Set a timer for 3 minutes. Sit or lie down with your eyes closed.

Breathe. Listen.

To your body. To your thoughts. To your emotions without judgement.

At the end, write down one sentence you heard ~ not from your mind, but from your *depth*.

Even if it makes no sense now ~ trust it.

Closing Mantra for the Today ~

"I listen with more than ears. I hear the voice of my becoming. I make space for my soul to speak."

April 17 – The Day of Devoted Choice

A story of sacred decision, soul direction, and the quiet power of choosing what aligns with who you're becoming

There once was a soul who feared choosing wrong.

They delayed decisions. Asked for signs. Waited until everything felt certain ~ which it never did.

What if they disappointed someone? What if the path they took closed another door forever?

They believed choices had to be perfect. Flawless. Unquestionable.

But one day ~ in the rising green of Northern spring, or the long amber drift of Southern autumn ~ the soul stood at a simple crossroads.

Neither direction was lit by neon certainty. But one felt… quiet. Rooted. Real.

They didn't feel sure. They felt *true*.

And with a breath that trembled and steadied all at once, they whispered:

"This is my choice ~ not because it's perfect, but because it's mine."

April 17 carries the energy of 8 (1 + 7), a number of power, alignment, and lived integrity. Today is about making a devoted choice ~ not to force certainty, but to walk with clarity and care.

It doesn't have to be dramatic. It doesn't need validation. It simply has to come from *you*.

The archetype of the day is The Soul Aligner ~ the self who doesn't chase the right path, but chooses a path that feels *real*, and then walks it with commitment.

Today's Symbols::

- A single stone laid in the middle of two paths, still and deliberate
- Garnet, for grounded decision-making and self-honoring intention
- The Lovers card, not just about connection ~ but conscious, value-based choosing
- A falcon, poised and ready, eyes fixed on the path ahead

Reflection Prompts:

- What choice have I been delaying out of fear of getting it wrong?
- What decision feels aligned ~ even if it's not easy, popular, or logical?

- Can I give myself permission to choose based on truth, not pressure?

Integration Practice: Declare One Choice

Today, name one small, honest decision you've been avoiding ~ and make it.

It could be:

- Saying no to an invitation
- Committing to a small habit that reflects your current truth
- Letting go of something you've been forcing

Write it down. Say it aloud. Then whisper:

"I trust this choice. I trust myself."

Let the act of choosing become a mirror of your self-respect.

Closing Mantra for the Today ~

"I do not wait for perfect clarity. I choose what feels aligned ~ and walk it with devotion."

April 18 – The Day of Inner Renewal

A story of quiet regeneration, the soul's soft reset, and the life that returns when you stop forcing and start allowing

There once was a soul who kept trying to fix themselves.

They read every book. Changed every habit. Rewrote their story ~ again and again.

But no matter how much they did, something always felt… unfinished.

One morning ~ as green buds reached quietly through Northern soil, or as trees shed their final gold in the Southern breeze ~ the soul woke and didn't do anything new.

They didn't journal. They didn't stretch. They didn't strive.

They just *breathed*.

And for the first time, the breath felt full.

Not because they had changed something ~ but because something *inside* them had begun again… *without effort*.

"Maybe I don't need to become," the soul whispered. "Maybe I'm just being renewed."

April 18 carries the energy of 9 (1 + 8), the number of spiritual integration, release, and completion ~ but not the end. This is the energy of clearing space *so that newness can find you again.*

Today is not about starting over. It's about allowing what's already trying to return.

The archetype of the day is The Soul Gardener ~ the part of you who doesn't plant from fear, but clears the weeds of old cycles and welcomes what wants to grow again ~ *naturally.*

Today's Symbols::

- A field after rain, quiet, rich, ready
- Chrysoprase, for heart-healing and emotional renewal
- The Death card, symbolic rebirth ~ not loss, but transformation
- A phoenix resting in ash, not rising yet, but whole again

Reflection Prompts:

- What part of me has quietly shifted in the background ~ and now wants to return?
- Where have I been trying to "fix" myself instead of allowing healing to happen?
- What if rest, stillness, or ease is the beginning of my next chapter ~ not the delay of it?

Integration Practice: The Renewal Breath

Find a quiet space.

Place both hands on your heart. Breathe in through your nose for 4 counts. Hold for 4. Exhale through your mouth for 6 counts.

Do this 3 times.

Then whisper:

"I allow myself to renew. I welcome what wants to return to life."

Today, do something gentle that feels like watering your spirit.

Closing Mantra for the Today ~

"I do not need to force what is already becoming. I allow space for renewal. I trust the life that rises in me again."

April 19 – The Day of Subtle Expansion

A story of gentle growth, invisible progress, and the quiet magic of becoming more without needing to be loud about it

There once was a soul who believed growth had to look like transformation.

Big steps. Big changes. Big shifts.

They waited for clarity to feel loud, for signs to be bold, for their becoming to be undeniable.

But what they didn't notice ~ not at first ~ was how often they were already expanding. In the way they paused before reacting. In the moment they chose rest over proving. In how they were starting to say *yes* to what felt aligned ~ and *no* without guilt.

One golden morning ~ as young trees reached upward in the North, or the final warmth lingered on falling leaves in the South ~ the soul touched a small plant in the garden.

It had grown. Just a little. But definitely more than yesterday.

And they realized:

"This is what it means to expand. Quietly. Naturally. Truly."

April 19 carries the energy of 1 (1 + 9 = 10 → 1), the number of initiation, unfolding identity, and soul-forward motion.

But this isn't the "new year" kind of energy. It's the kind that says, *You're already growing ~ just look closer.*

The archetype of the day is The Quiet Riser ~ the soul who expands without applause, who trusts their small wins, and who honors every inch of inner stretch.

Today's Symbols::

- A sprout pushing through soil, still curled, still tender, yet undeniably alive
- Green aventurine, for confidence in soft growth and heart-led expansion
- The Seven of Pentacles, tending slow growth with patience
- A snail, moving forward gently, no rush ~ but always in motion

Reflection Prompts:

- Where have I been growing in ways I haven't acknowledged?
- What small shift in my thoughts, habits, or heart has made a difference lately?

- Can I celebrate progress without needing it to be impressive?

Integration Practice: The 1% Recognition

Write down three things you've done in the past two weeks that reflect even the slightest growth.

Examples:

- "I responded with more patience than usual."
- "I honored my need for quiet without guilt."
- "I said no when it was hard."

Whisper to yourself:

"This counts. I am expanding."

Then move through today with the awareness that growth doesn't always bloom ~ sometimes, it *breathes*.

Closing Mantra for the Today ~

"I grow in the quiet. I expand with ease. Even the smallest stretch is sacred."

April 20 – The Day of Grounded Becoming

A story of embodied presence, practical wisdom, and allowing yourself to evolve at the pace of real life

There once was a soul who loved transformation.

They dreamed of radical change. Longed to feel different. Craved the rush of becoming something new.

But the journey kept pulling them back into the mundane. The dishes. The bills. The body aches. They wondered why their evolution felt so… ordinary.

Then one morning ~ as the earth warmed in the North and turned cooler in the South ~ the soul stepped outside barefoot and felt the soil beneath them.

Not metaphor. Not magic. Just real ground ~ holding them.

In that moment, they understood:

"Becoming isn't always a breakthrough. Sometimes, it's simply being here differently."

Not floating above life. But moving through it ~ grounded, true, *alive*.

April 20 marks the beginning of Taurus season and holds the energy of 2 (2 + 0), symbolizing inner balance, rooted stability, and embodied choice.

Today is an invitation to move beyond conceptual growth ~ and into *lived growth*.

It's time to take what you know and give it form. To root your becoming in the body, the calendar, the *ground you stand on*.

The archetype of the day is The Grounded Soul ~ the self who builds rather than chases, who honors their evolution in quiet, steady steps.

Today's Symbols::

— Bare feet on cool soil, steady and connected
— Red jasper, for grounding, physical integration, and slow momentum
— The Empress, thriving through embodiment, nourishment, and life-force
— A tortoise, moving with ancient confidence and unapologetic pacing

Reflection Prompts:

— What have I already embodied ~ no longer just a belief, but a lived truth?
— Where do I need to slow down and ground ~ so my becoming can take root?

- What rhythms help me stay connected to my body, my life, my now?

Integration Practice: One Grounded Action

Choose one small, concrete action today that honors the version of you that's emerging.

It could be:

- Cleaning a space with love
- Cooking a nourishing meal
- Updating your calendar with your true priorities
- Going outside barefoot to reconnect with earth

Then say aloud:

"I am not becoming in theory. I am becoming in reality."

Let your body feel it. Let the earth hold it.

Closing Mantra for the Today ~

"I root into the truth of who I am. My becoming is grounded, steady, and real."

April 21 – The Day of Sacred Self-Belief

A story of inner trust, quiet self-honoring, and the moment you decide to believe in yourself ~ not for approval, but for alignment

There once was a soul who waited to be chosen.

They waited for someone to see their worth. To validate their voice. To confirm what they already knew ~ but didn't yet trust.

Each day they showed up, gave more, tried harder. But the recognition never quite arrived in the way they hoped.

Until one morning ~ as the Northern world blossomed in full color, or the Southern world softened into gold and gray ~ the soul stood before a mirror.

No audience. No applause.

Just them.

And in that silence, something ancient whispered:

"You are the one who must believe first."

So they did. Not perfectly. Not permanently.

But *enough* to take the next step. And that… changed everything.

April 21 holds the energy of 3 (2 + 1), the number of expression, personal truth, and radiant self-ownership. Today calls you into sacred self-belief ~ not the loud, performative kind, but the rooted kind that says:

"I am worthy, because I exist."

The archetype of the day is The Inner Believer ~ the part of you that affirms your own light before the world reflects it back. The part that chooses worth, not as a reward, but as a *birthright*.

Today's Symbols::

- A candle lit in front of a mirror, soft and steady
- Citrine, for confidence, personal power, and radiant truth
- The Queen of Wands, unapologetically radiant, rooted in self-trust
- A lioness, not needing to prove ~ only needing to *be*

Reflection Prompts:

- Where have I been waiting for permission to trust myself?
- What would shift in me today if I decided to believe I'm already enough?
- What part of me longs to be seen ~ and can I begin by seeing it myself?

Integration Practice: The Mirror Declaration

Stand in front of a mirror. Look into your own eyes. Place one hand on your heart.

Say aloud (even if it feels strange at first):

"I believe in who I am becoming. I trust my voice, my path, and my light. I am already enough."

Repeat it three times. Let your own gaze be the reflection you've been waiting for.

Closing Mantra for the Today ~

"I no longer wait to be chosen. I choose myself ~ with reverence, not ego. I believe in me."

April 22 – The Day of Earth-Rooted Wisdom

A story of ancient knowing, ecological presence, and remembering that your soul is not separate from the soil beneath your feet

There once was a soul who felt ungrounded.

They floated through life with ideas and inspiration, but little connection to rhythm, ritual, or root.

They admired the stars but forgot the soil.

Then one afternoon ~ as spring's greening crowned the Northern trees, or autumn's gold blanketed the Southern hills ~ they walked barefoot across the earth.

Not for steps. Not for steps tracked. But to feel.

Each footfall reminded them:

"You are not above this. You belong to it."

And just like that, the soul remembered:

Their body was a part of the earth ~ a vessel of the same wisdom, cycles, and sacred slowness.

They were not floating anymore. They were *returning*.

April 22 holds the energy of 4 (2 + 2), the number of structure, grounding, and embodied wisdom. It is also Earth Day ~ a global moment of ecological reverence.

Today is a reminder: Your soul doesn't just rise toward the divine ~ it *roots into the earth*.

The archetype of the day is The Earth-Touched Mystic ~ the part of you that seeks spirituality not only in transcendence, but in dirt, plants, trees, breath, and body.

Today's Symbols::

- A circle of stones surrounding a seedling, protected and growing
- Petrified wood, for ancestral grounding and earth memory
- The Ace of Pentacles, symbolizing new roots, grounded potential, and practical magic
- A tree frog, still on a leaf ~ soft, silent, sacred

Reflection Prompts:

- How can I root myself more deeply into the rhythms of nature today?

- Where have I been seeking growth upward ~ instead of downward, into soul and soil?
- What wisdom does the earth hold for the season I'm in?

Integration Practice: Earth Connection Ritual

Today, connect directly with the natural world ~ not to escape, but to return.

Ideas:

- Walk barefoot on grass or soil
- Sit with your back against a tree
- Tend to a garden or houseplant in mindful silence
- Touch a stone or shell and breathe with it for one full minute

As you do, whisper:

"I remember where I come from. I root into what is real."

Let this moment be your soul's reunion with the earth.

Closing Mantra for the Today ~

"I am not separate from this world. The soil, the stone, the sky ~ all live in me. I walk in rhythm with the living earth."

April 23 – The Day of Sacred Boundaries

A story of self-respect, quiet protection, and the soul-deep knowing that saying no is a profound act of love

There once was a soul who gave and gave… and gave.

They said yes to stay connected. They said yes to be seen as kind. They said yes because saying no felt like abandonment ~ or worse, failure.

But over time, they felt stretched thin. Their joy dimmed. Their energy fractured.

One evening ~ as the Northern skies turned pink with spring, or the Southern dusk gathered into quiet grey ~ the soul sat alone and placed a hand over their chest.

A single, clear whisper arose:

"You're allowed to protect your peace."

It wasn't a shout. It didn't come from anger.

It came from love ~ for the parts of themselves they'd been sacrificing for too long.

April 23 carries the energy of 5 (2 + 3), the number of freedom, boundaries, and recalibration.

Today isn't about walls. It's about wise thresholds.

It's about choosing what enters your space ~ and what doesn't. Not as rejection. But as *self-honoring direction*.

The archetype of the day is The Boundary Keeper ~ the part of you who protects what is sacred, and who knows that saying no to what drains you is saying yes to your highest alignment.

Today's Symbols::

- A circle drawn in salt, unbroken and luminous
- Black tourmaline, for energetic protection and boundary clarity
- The Nine of Pentacles, self-resourced, graceful, and discerning
- A hedgehog, curled but not afraid ~ simply aware of what is safe and what is not

Reflection Prompts:

- Where in my life am I overextending out of guilt, not love?
- What boundary would protect my peace ~ even if it disappoints someone?
- What if "no" is not rejection, but an act of radical self-care?

Integration Practice: The Sacred "No" Letter

Write a short, private note to yourself beginning with:

"I release the pressure to say yes when my body says no."

Follow it with:

"I am allowed to..." "I no longer owe..." "I choose to protect..."

This is not a confrontation. It is a reclamation.

Fold it. Keep it. Or tear it into the wind. Let your voice become your boundary.

Closing Mantra for the Today ~

"My peace is precious. I protect what nourishes me. I honor myself with every no I speak in truth."

April 24 – The Day of Soul Recognition

A story of inner sight, sacred remembering, and the quiet moment you finally see yourself clearly ~ and choose to stay

There once was a soul who became skilled at hiding.

Not from others ~ but from themselves.

They wore masks to keep the peace. They shape-shifted to fit in. They spoke in tones that pleased, but never fully resonated.

Over time, they forgot what they looked like underneath it all.

Then one still morning ~ as light broke softly through Northern leaves, or the Southern wind paused in reverence ~ the soul stood in front of a mirror they hadn't dared look into for some time.

Not to fix. Not to analyze.

Just to witness.

And in the reflection, there wasn't perfection. But there was presence.

"Oh," the soul whispered. "There you are."

April 24 holds the energy of 6 (2 + 4), the number of harmony, integration, and soulful self-awareness.

This is a day not to improve ~ but to *remember*. To look at yourself fully and say:

"I see you. I know you. I'm staying."

The archetype of the day is The Soul Witness ~ the part of you who no longer seeks a version of yourself to perform, but one to *embrace*. The one who recognizes the layers, the truth, and the beauty that lives beyond image.

Today's Symbols::

- A mirror placed in sunlight, glowing, clear, undistorted
- Lapis lazuli, for truth, self-awareness, and inner sight
- The Judgement card, not as critique, but as awakening ~ a rising into one's full name
- A swan, seeing its reflection in still water, unstartled ~ only whole

Reflection Prompts:

- What part of myself have I been avoiding ~ and what would it mean to finally acknowledge it?
- Where have I been waiting for someone else to see me ~ and how can I offer that to myself first?

- What does it feel like to be fully witnessed ~ even by just one person (even if that person is me)?

Integration Practice: The Recognition Note

Write a note to yourself today beginning with:

"Today, I recognize…"

Continue the sentence in whatever way feels honest:

- "…how far I've come."
- "…my resilience in hard moments."
- "…the softness I've protected."
- "…my strength in staying."

Reread it aloud. Let it land. Let it light something within.

This is the beginning of deeper self-seeing.

Closing Mantra for the Today ~

"I see myself ~ clearly, gently, fully. I do not look away. I am whole as I am."

April 25 – The Day of Quiet Devotion

A story of sacred attention, steady care, and the kind of love that shows up not once ~ but again and again, without needing to be seen

There once was a soul who thought devotion had to be loud.

They looked for grand gestures. Declarations. Fireworks of faith.

But those moments, though beautiful, were fleeting.

One dusk ~ as petals opened to the lengthening light in the North, or as leaves cradled golden quiet in the South ~ the soul noticed something else.

The way they always lit a candle at the same hour. The way they checked in on a friend without fail. The way they returned to their breath when no one was watching.

These weren't grand. They were *devoted*.

"Maybe devotion," the soul whispered, "is not what I do once ~ but what I choose *repeatedly*."

In stillness. In rhythm. In love.

April 25 carries the energy of 7 (2 + 5), the number of inner truth, spiritual focus, and quiet alignment.

Today is an invitation to reframe devotion ~ not as performance, but as presence. Not as effort, but *return*.

The archetype of the day is The Devoted Flame ~ the self who tends sacredness not through drama, but consistency. The one who keeps coming back to what matters, gently, no matter what.

Today's Symbols::

- A single flame burning in a clay holder, unshaken by wind
- Selenite, for purity, spiritual devotion, and energetic simplicity
- The Eight of Pentacles, showing up to the craft of soul work, with love
- A turtledove, nesting in the same place year after year ~ not out of duty, but care

Reflection Prompts:

- What do I return to ~ not out of obligation, but love?
- What small daily act feels like an offering to my soul?
- What would it look like to treat one part of my day with quiet reverence?

Integration Practice: Create a Small Devotion

Today, choose one tiny ritual to perform with full attention and intention.

Ideas:

— Brew tea slowly, without distraction.
— Light a candle and sit for 3 minutes in silence.
— Water a plant with a whispered thank you.
— Write one sentence of gratitude and fold it into a jar.

Let this action be your *return* ~ to yourself, to simplicity, to what matters most.

Closing Mantra for the Today ~

"I return to what I love. I return to what grounds me. My devotion is not noise ~ it is presence."

April 26 – The Day of Unshakable Calm

A story of inner steadiness, quiet confidence, and discovering the peace that doesn't depend on your circumstances

There once was a soul who was always bracing.

Waiting for the next wave. Preparing for the next fall. Living in quiet anticipation of things going wrong.

They were strong, yes ~ but tired. Always scanning. Always on alert.

Then one day ~ as rain kissed the buds of the Northern spring, or winds settled across the cooling fields of the South ~ the soul sat by still water.

No rush. No noise. No urgency.

And they felt it ~ the kind of peace that didn't ask questions, didn't chase answers.

It simply *was*.

"What if I could live like this inside?" they whispered. "What if calm isn't what happens when life settles ~ but what rises when *I* do?"

April 26 carries the energy of 8 (2 + 6), the number of strength, inner mastery, and grounded presence. But today's strength isn't rigid ~ it's fluid and steady.

This is a day to meet chaos ~ external or internal ~ with *unshakable calm.*

The archetype of the day is The Inner Anchor ~ the part of you that stays rooted even in the storm, not because it resists emotion, but because it trusts your center.

Today's Symbols::

— A rock in the middle of a river, unmoved as the current flows around it
— Blue lace agate, for calm communication and nervous system soothing
— The Strength card, not of force ~ but of gentle, grounded confidence
— A sea turtle, slow and ancient, carrying peace across long distances

Reflection Prompts:

— What do I believe I need before I can feel calm ~ and is that actually true?
— What helps me return to steadiness when life gets loud?

- What if calm isn't something I find, but something I already carry?

Integration Practice: The Calm Reset

Throughout today, when tension arises, pause and take a 3-breath reset:

- Inhale for 4 counts
- Hold for 4 counts
- Exhale slowly for 6–8 counts

Repeat this three times. Place a hand on your chest or stomach. Whisper:

"I return to calm. I am safe here."

Let this be your anchor. Again and again.

Closing Mantra for the Today ~

"I carry calm within me. I am the stillness beneath the noise. I return to my center ~ and rest there."

April 27 – The Day of Authentic Expression

A story of honest voice, creative freedom, and letting the world meet the truest version of who you really are

There once was a soul who edited everything.

Their words. Their laughter. Their dreams.

They said what was safe. They wore what was acceptable. They shared what was "just enough" ~ never too much.

Until one morning ~ as wildflowers opened across Northern meadows, or fallen leaves gathered in quiet Southern corners ~ the soul picked up a pen, dipped a brush, opened their mouth…

And didn't filter.

They didn't think about how it would be received. They let it come out messy, raw, vibrant, *real*.

And in that moment, they didn't just express. They *existed*.

"This is what I sound like. This is what I feel like," they whispered. "This is me ~ not a version. Not a role. Just… me."

April 27 carries the energy of 9 (2 + 7), the number of culmination, creative offering, and personal release. Today is an invitation to express yourself *without editing your soul*.

This is not about performance. It's about presence through expression ~ honest, heartfelt, and unpolished if it needs to be.

The archetype of the day is The Soul Voice ~ the self who speaks, sings, writes, creates, or simply shows up in a way that honors what is true, not just what is palatable.

Today's Symbols::

- A canvas with bold, unrefined strokes, layered in color
- Carnelian, for courage, creativity, and vocal confidence
- The Knight of Wands, spirited, expressive, willing to risk being fully seen
- A mockingbird, singing its own mix of borrowed and original songs ~ joyful, fearless

Reflection Prompts:

- Where have I been holding back my full expression ~ and why?
- What would I say or create today if I wasn't trying to be perfect?
- How can I meet the world honestly, even if just in one sentence or action?

Integration Practice: Express Without Editing

Choose one medium today ~ writing, speaking, movement, drawing, singing ~ and let something come through unfiltered.

No audience. No pressure. No polishing.

Just presence.

Afterward, place your hand on your heart and say:

"That was mine. That was true."

Let this become a ritual of self-recognition.

Closing Mantra for the Today ~

"I no longer hide behind roles. I express who I am ~ not to impress, but to be whole."

April 28 – The Day of Soulful Connection

A story of deep presence with others, heart-led relating, and the sacred recognition that real connection begins with being fully seen

There once was a soul who craved connection ~ but felt alone in every room.

They made small talk. Smiled on cue. Played the part of someone "easy to be around."

But something was always missing. A layer untouched. A truth unspoken.

Then one twilight ~ as the Northern sky turned lavender with spring, or the Southern earth exhaled into deeper dusk ~ the soul looked someone in the eye and didn't pretend.

They said, "This is what I'm really feeling." And stayed. Soft. Honest. Unpolished.

And to their surprise… they weren't rejected.

They were *met*.

"Real connection," the soul realized, "doesn't come from being agreeable. It comes from being *real*."

April 28 carries the energy of 1 (2 + 8 = 10 → 1), the number of authentic initiation, vulnerable sharing, and true relational presence.

Today is about more than communication ~ it's about soulful connection: the kind that requires courage, clarity, and a willingness to be fully seen *as you are*.

The archetype of the day is The Open-Hearted Mirror ~ the part of you that meets others from wholeness, not performance, and invites honesty as the pathway to depth.

Today's Symbols::

- Two hands gently joined over a candle, light shared but not forced
- Rose quartz, for compassion, self-honoring relationships, and tender truth
- The Two of Cups, the exchange of souls beyond masks or roles
- A pair of dolphins, surfacing together ~ different, but moving in rhythm

Reflection Prompts:

- Where am I longing for more depth in my relationships ~ and what truth have I not yet spoken?

- What part of me am I still hiding from others ~ and what might happen if I shared it?
- How can I create connection today by being more fully myself, not more agreeable?

Integration Practice: Share One Honest Moment

Choose someone in your life today ~ a friend, partner, coworker, or even a stranger ~ and offer one small piece of truth or presence that goes beneath the surface.

Examples:

- "I really appreciated what you said the other day. It stayed with me."
- "I've been feeling overwhelmed lately, and I just needed to say it out loud."
- "Here's something about me I don't always share…"

Let it be imperfect. Let it be real.

Then notice how it feels ~ not how it's received, but how it *frees* you.

Closing Mantra for the Today ~

"I connect by showing up fully. I offer my truth. I receive others with care. I am worthy of being known."

April 29 – The Day of Embodied Grace

A story of quiet dignity, soulful movement, and honoring the wisdom that lives within your body and how you carry yourself through the world

There once was a soul who thought grace was something you had to earn.

They imagined it belonged to those who never stumbled, who always knew what to say, who moved through life with effortless elegance.

But the soul's path was clumsy. Messy. Filled with pauses, detours, and days that didn't flow.

They called themselves "awkward," "behind," "not graceful enough."

Until one morning ~ as the spring winds danced across the Northern fields, or the leaves twirled gently in the Southern air ~ the soul moved slowly, without correction, and noticed something new:

Every step they took ~ even the uneven ones ~ was part of a rhythm.

"Grace," the soul realized, "is not perfection. Grace is how I keep showing up ~ body, breath, and all."

April 29 carries the energy of 2 (2 + 9 = 11 → 1 + 1 = 2), the number of balance, embodiment, and relational flow.

Today is an invitation to move with embodied grace ~ not performative polish, but deep attunement to your pace, your posture, your presence.

The archetype of the day is The Soul Dancer ~ the self who learns not to resist life's rhythm, but to move with it ~ tenderly, imperfectly, fully.

Today's Symbols::

- A single feather falling into still water, light and intentional
- Moonstone, for fluidity, intuition, and graceful integration
- The Temperance card, the alchemy of patience, flow, and sacred pacing
- A cat, stretching slowly before it moves ~ unhurried, elegant in instinct

Reflection Prompts:

- What does "grace" mean to me ~ and who taught me that?

- How can I move through my day with more softness and less strain?
- Where have I been hard on my body, my rhythm, or my pace ~ and what would it feel like to forgive that?

Integration Practice: Move with Awareness

Choose one physical action today ~ walking, stretching, reaching, rising ~ and perform it with complete awareness.

Slow. Intentional. Present.

Feel the muscles, the breath, the motion.

Then say silently:

"This, too, is grace."

Let your body be the meditation ~ not the problem to fix.

Closing Mantra for the Today ~

"I move in harmony with myself. Grace lives in my breath, my pauses, my pace. I do not need to be perfect ~ I only need to be present."

April 30 – The Day of Integration

*A story of inner weaving,
soulful synthesis, and
honoring how far you've come
~ not in distance, but in depth*

There once was a soul who kept starting over.

New intentions. New tools. New beginnings.

But every time they felt close to clarity, they'd wipe the slate clean. Afraid that their progress wasn't pure enough. That they hadn't done it "right."

Then one golden evening ~ as Northern trees shimmered in fresh leaves, or the Southern earth curled into soft quiet ~ the soul looked back, not in regret, but in reverence.

They saw not scattered fragments ~ but threads.

Moments of courage. Choices made in faith. Tiny shifts that had woven a deeper truth.

"I am not starting over," the soul whispered. "I am gathering who I've been ~ and *becoming whole.*"

April 30 carries the energy of 3 (3 + 0), the number of synthesis, expression, and realized wisdom. It's a sacred moment of integration ~ the soul's invitation to stop discarding and start *weaving*.

Today is about honoring everything you've lived ~ not as broken pieces, but as *part of your becoming*.

The archetype of the day is The Integrator ~ the self who sees the connections beneath the chaos, who welcomes every version of themselves to the present moment, and who walks forward carrying the full truth.

Today's Symbols::

- A woven tapestry with mismatched threads, beautiful in its realness
- Fluorite, for integration, clarity, and unifying the many parts of self
- The World card, completion, wholeness, and return to center
- A butterfly, landing for a moment ~ wings closed, resting in fullness

Reflection Prompts:

- What part of me have I tried to leave behind ~ but now realize is still part of my journey?
- What lesson or insight from this month deserves to be carried forward?

- How can I move from "fixing" into "integrating" ~ with grace?

Integration Practice: Thread the Story

Today, create a visual or written reflection of the month:

- Draw a spiral and write one insight from each week around its edges
- Or write a paragraph beginning with:

"This month taught me…"

Then place your hand on your heart and say:

"I welcome every part of this path. Nothing is wasted. I am whole."

Let this be your ritual of closing ~ and continuity.

Closing Mantra for the Today ~

"I am not fragmented. I am a living thread of everything I've walked through. I carry it all with reverence ~ into what's next."

April Reflection

The Rhythm of Opening

You've just moved through 30 days of emergence. Not explosive growth ~ but subtle becoming. Not declarations ~ but decisions. Not breakthroughs ~ but revealed breath.

April was never asking for performance. It asked for presence ~ in your choices, your rhythms, your unfolding truths.

And as you reach the final page of this month, pause to acknowledge:

You didn't just read. You opened ~ even if quietly.

Remember Where You Began

Look back to April 1 ~ The Day of Hidden Blooming. Can you still feel the quiet readiness? The seed just beneath the surface?

Now, revisit April 30 ~ The Day of Integration. See the arc? Not a line, but a spiral ~ from unseen potential to embodied becoming.

And yet, they're connected.

Like January 1 ~ The Day of Sacred Beginning, this month ends much like it began: in stillness, truth, and soft direction.

Noticing the Numbers

- The 1s (April 1, 10, 19) spoke of *becoming, self-initiation*, and *soul alignment*. ➤ Did you also feel echoes from January's 1s ~ moments when you were asked to begin again, differently?
- The 2s (April 2, 11, 20, 29) brought you into *emotional attunement* and *embodied presence*. ➤ Compare with February 2, 11, 20 ~ a thread of *honesty and tenderness* weaves through them.
- The 7s (April 7, 16, 25) invited trust, *inner calm*, and *devotion*. ➤ These days echoed the deep inner listening of March 7 and 16 ~ a continuity of inner guidance.

Can you trace your own rhythm of growth through these repeated numerological energies?

Monthly Journal Invitations

Use the prompts below to deepen your April integration. You may write into your journal, sketch, or speak them aloud ~ in the form of memory, prayer, or poem.

— Emotional Blooming

What opened in me this month ~ even if no one else saw it? What emotional truth am I now more willing to speak?

— Soulful Practice

What new rhythm or ritual began to take root? Which gentle action brought me closer to my own voice?

— Inner Witness

What part of me surprised me ~ in tenderness, power, or honesty? Who have I become more aligned with: myself, another, or something higher?

— Energetic Echo

Which day from a previous month rose again this month ~ with a new message, meaning, or depth? (You might revisit January 17, February 11, or March 25.)

— Next Season's Seed

What soul lesson from April do I want to carry into May ~ not to solve, but to nurture further?

Optional Journal Template Structure

(Use as often as you like)

- Date of Reflection:
- Today I remember…
- What surprised me this month…
- Where I felt most real…
- A practice I want to continue…
- A message I still carry from earlier months…
- What I'm planting for May…

Final Reflection

You are not behind. You are not unfinished.

You are mid-bloom. Mid-sentence. Mid-spirit.

And you are doing it all ~ with grace, rhythm, and devotion.

Let April's unfolding meet May's expansion.

You are not the same soul who began this month.

You are becoming ~ beautifully, quietly, wholly.

May 1 – The Day of Inner Blooming

A story of emotional opening, sensual trust, and the slow unfolding of intimacy ~ with oneself and with another

There once was a soul who had closed like a flower after too much storm.

Not all at once. A little each time they were misunderstood. A little each time they reached for connection and were met with absence.

They still smiled. Still gave. But the petals inside them had curled tight.

Then one morning ~ as May light stretched across the Northern horizon, or crisp leaves fell gently in the South ~ the soul lay beside their partner, and for the first time in a long time… they didn't hide.

Not their body. Not their breath. Not their fear.

There was no grand gesture. Just the closeness of skin. The warmth of hands. The kind of silence that says, *I'm still here. And I see you.*

"Maybe blooming," the soul whispered, "isn't something I do alone. Maybe I open because someone stays."

May 1 carries the energy of 1, the number of emergence and identity ~ not as a performance, but as *permission*.

Today isn't about becoming more. It's about unfolding safely ~ with your own heart, and perhaps, in the arms of another.

The archetype of the day is The Sacred Bloom ~ the self who is no longer striving to grow, but allowing themselves to soften, to open, and to be *held while blooming*.

Today's Symbols::

- A rose partially open, kissed by early light
- Rose quartz, for heart-led connection and tender trust
- The Lovers card, not for passion alone ~ but for sacred reflection and mirrored truth
- Two foxes lying side by side, tails touching, completely still and safe

Reflection Prompts:

- Where in my life am I ready to open again ~ emotionally, sensually, or spiritually?
- What does blooming with another person look like for me ~ and what does it require?
- Can I let someone near without losing myself? Can I stay present in that nearness?

Integration Practice: The Trust Touch

If you're with a partner:

- Spend a few minutes today touching without agenda ~ hands, backs, faces.
- Let it be slow. Let it be real. No performance, just presence.

If you're solo:

- Place one hand over your heart and one over your belly.
- Say softly:

"I am opening. I am safe. I am held ~ by myself, by life, by love."

This is not just emotional blooming. It is sensual safety. It is soul permission.

Closing Mantra for the Today ~

"I bloom not to be seen ~ but to be felt. My softness is my courage. My opening is sacred."

May 2 – The Day of Soulful Invitation

A story of emotional intimacy, sacred approach, and the quiet magic of saying "I want to know you" ~ with your presence, not just your words

There once was a soul who longed to be invited in.

Not just welcomed. *Wanted.* Not out of obligation ~ but desire.

They had known connection that was surface-deep. Touch that reached the skin, but never the spirit. They had known being kissed without being *seen*.

But one evening ~ as the May moon lifted over the Northern trees, or the Southern winds cooled the quiet landscape ~ the soul sat with their partner, and something shifted.

They didn't ask for anything. They didn't reach. They *waited* ~ not in fear, but in sacred offering.

And when their partner looked up and whispered, *"Can I come closer?"* Something opened in both of them ~ deeper than skin. It was an *invitation*, not a request.

"This," the soul whispered, "is what it feels like to be chosen ~ not just touched."

May 2 carries the energy of 2, the number of sacred relationship, mirrored truth, and emotional reciprocity.

Today invites you to explore the difference between closeness that is *habitual* and closeness that is intentional.

The archetype of the day is The Inviter ~ the self who opens space for intimacy through presence, permission, and *reverence* ~ not urgency.

This is a day of sacred approach.

Today's Symbols::

- A door ajar with candlelight glowing from within, warm and welcoming
- Pink chalcedony, for openness, communication, and emotional resonance
- The Two of Cups, a connection built not just on love ~ but *attunement*
- A crane bowing to another, in slow, elegant courtship

Reflection Prompts:

- Where do I long to be invited in ~ not just physically, but emotionally or energetically?
- What does it feel like when someone approaches me with care, not expectation?

- How can I invite someone into deeper connection ~ without needing to be in control?

Integration Practice: The Invitation Moment

With a partner:

- Tonight, create a space of intentional stillness.
- Without initiating touch, look into their eyes and ask:

"What would feel like connection to you right now?"

- Let whatever arises come without judgment ~ even silence.

Alone:

- Journal a letter to yourself titled:

"You are invited to…"

- Fill the page with gentle permissions:

"You are invited to rest. To desire. To speak. To receive."

This is how soulful intimacy begins: Not with taking ~ but with inviting.

Closing Mantra for the Today ~

"I invite closeness with care. I enter sacred space with presence. I am worthy of being wanted, not just received."

May 3 – The Day of Emotional Undress

A story of tenderness, brave vulnerability, and the deep intimacy that happens when hearts are exposed more.

There once was a soul who thought intimacy lived in the body.

And yes, they had known closeness ~ Skin to skin, kiss to kiss, hands in movement.

But something had always been missing.

Afterwards, they often felt hollow. Not because touch was wrong ~ but because *truth* was missing.

Then one night ~ as the Northern air warmed in spring's hush, or the Southern sky turned burnt-orange with early dusk ~ the soul sat undressed beside their partner.

But this time, it wasn't about seduction.

They wept.

Not for pain, but for *release*. A letting go of shame. Of old armor. Of the need to be composed.

Their partner stayed. No fixing. No pity. Just… staying.

"This," the soul thought, "is what it means to be *naked*."

May 3 carries the energy of 3, the number of expression, heart-truth, and soulful communication.

Today is not about sexual performance ~ it's about emotional presence. The kind that happens when we choose to be seen in our softness ~ *and stay open*.

The archetype of the day is The Tender Mirror ~ the self who does not hide behind polished surfaces, but meets another (or themselves) with honesty, compassion, and brave exposure.

Today's Symbols::

- A sheer curtain pulled back from a sunlit window, revealing the room inside
- Morganite, for emotional softness, trauma release, and relational healing
- The Three of Cups, not just joy ~ but safe, vulnerable celebration of shared truth
- A pair of swans, necks touching gently, eyes closed ~ no urgency, only trust

Reflection Prompts:

- What emotional truth have I been covering ~ even in my closest relationships?
- What fear rises when I imagine being fully seen ~ not physically, but emotionally?

- Where in my body do I hold that fear ~ and what would it feel like to let it melt, even a little?

Integration Practice: Undress with Intention

With a partner:

- Share an experience of vulnerability ~ a moment you felt ashamed, exposed, or afraid.
- As you undress (if that's shared space today), do so slowly and with reverence ~ naming one thing you release with each layer.

Solo:

- Stand before a mirror and slowly remove an item of clothing.
- With each layer, say:

"I release the need to hide…" "I allow myself to be seen…"
Even without a witness, your soul listens.

Closing Mantra for the Today ~

"I am safe in my softness. I do not need to hide to be held. My vulnerability is not weakness ~ it is sacred truth."

May 4 – The Day of Erotic Presence

A story of awakened touch, sacred heat, and the full-body remembering that pleasure is not performance ~ it is presence

There once was a soul who had experienced desire ~ but rarely felt safe inside it.

They had learned to give. To satisfy. To be beautiful on cue.

But when it came to their own pleasure ~ their own longing ~ they quieted.

Desire had become something they *offered*, not something they *owned*.

Then one slow morning ~ as the Northern sun rose thick with scent, or the Southern light turned gold and slanted ~ the soul traced their fingers over their own skin without flinching.

There was no rush. No agenda. No waiting to be received.

And later, when they met their partner's eyes in silence, it wasn't a question. It was a statement:

"I am here. In this body. In this moment. With nothing to hide."

And their partner didn't reach ~ not yet. They *matched the presence*.

Together, they breathed.

And together, they *remembered*.

May 4 carries the energy of 4, the number of grounded embodiment, stability, and sacred structure.

Today isn't about fantasy or indulgence. It is about erotic truth ~ the kind that lives in sensation, breath, eyes, and nearness without demand.

The archetype of the day is The Erotic Witness ~ the self who shows up in the moment with nothing to perform, nothing to chase, and everything to *feel*.

Today's Symbols::

- A silk cloth laid over sun-warmed skin, soft and weightless
- Red garnet, for passion, grounded sensuality, and heart-rooted intimacy
- The Ace of Wands, new spark, creative fire, and embodied invitation
- Two panthers resting together, alert but still, every muscle listening

Reflection Prompts:

- What part of my sensuality have I muted ~ and what would it mean to let it rise?

- Can I be present with desire ~ without rushing it, explaining it, or performing it?
- What happens in my body when I slow down enough to feel what's really there?

Integration Practice: Erotic Stillness

With a partner:

- Sit or lie close without touching.
- Breathe together. Hold eye contact.
- Let desire build *without acting*.
- Whisper:

"I am here. I feel this. I do not need to rush."

Alone:

- Explore your body slowly, not to reach an end, but to meet yourself.
- Light a candle. Trace your skin. Pause. Stay present.
- Say:

"My pleasure is sacred. My body is listening."

This is not about climax. It is about *contact* ~ real, raw, reverent.

Closing Mantra for the Today ~

"I am fully here. My presence is enough. Desire lives in the sacred rhythm of my body."

May 5 – The Day of Vulnerable Union

A story of shared surrender, intimate safety, and the soul-deep connection that arises when two people meet without armor

There once was a soul who had learned how to merge ~ physically.

They knew how to move in sync. To kiss with practiced rhythm. To give what was expected ~ and receive just enough to survive.

But inside, a deeper part of them remained untouched.

Not the body. But the *being*.

Then one quiet night ~ as the Northern stars appeared in full spring bloom, or the Southern air cooled into tender dark ~ they lay beside their partner, skin to skin, heart to heart.

There were no words. Only breath.

And then, one whispered truth ~ the kind you only say when your body feels safe enough to open your soul:

"I'm afraid to need you. But I do."

And instead of pulling away… their partner *stayed*.

Not to fix, but to *feel* ~ and to hold them, fully.

That night wasn't about sex. It was about union ~ where hearts were exposed, and everything else followed naturally.

May 5 carries the double resonance of 5 ~ change, freedom, emotional movement, and sacred surrender.

Today is about vulnerable union ~ not forced fusion, but chosen closeness, built from presence, safety, and truth.

The archetype of the day is The Soul Companion ~ the one who doesn't just share a bed or a breath, but a moment of *realness* ~ where no one hides and no one pretends.

Today's Symbols::

- Two naked figures resting forehead to forehead, neither reaching, just resting
- Kunzite, for emotional vulnerability, trust, and gentle connection
- The Two of Pentacles, harmonizing emotion and body, navigating togetherness in real time
- A pair of wolves curled around one another, silent and synchronized

Reflection Prompts:

- What do I withhold in moments of intimacy ~ not from fear of rejection, but fear of being too much?

- What would it feel like to let my guard down, not to be saved ~ but simply to be held?
- Where can I allow myself to need ~ and still feel strong?

Integration Practice: The Heart Confession

With a partner:

- During or after physical closeness, speak one sentence that reveals emotional truth.
    - Not about the act.
    - About your *inner experience.*

Examples:

"I feel safest with you when you breathe with me." "Sometimes I'm afraid to be this close ~ but I want to be." "This kind of softness scares me... but it also heals me."

Alone:

- Journal a confession to your future or inner beloved.
- Title it: *"Here's what I want you to know when we're this close..."*
- Let yourself write what you never say.

Closing Mantra for the Today ~

"I meet you without masks. I let myself be known in my softness. This is union ~ where nothing is forced, and everything is real."

May 6 – The Day of Shared Breath

A story of rhythm, sacred slowness, and the soul-deep intimacy found in the space between inhale and exhale

There once was a soul who had rushed through love.

Not out of carelessness ~ but fear. They had learned that to slow down might mean to feel too much. That stillness might uncover longing, or pain, or depth they weren't sure they could hold.

So they moved quickly ~ even in intimacy. Quick to undress. Quick to please. Quick to retreat.

But one morning ~ as the Northern sky softened into a blanket of early light, or the Southern air thickened with golden stillness ~ they awoke beside their partner.

Nothing stirred. No words passed. Only breath ~ slow, warm, steady.

And without realizing, they matched it.

Two chests, rising and falling. Not touching. Just *tuning*.

And in that breath ~ *shared and silent* ~ they felt closer than in any kiss.

"This," the soul realized, "is what intimacy sounds like when no one is speaking."

May 6 carries the energy of 6, the number of harmony, attunement, and the shared pulse of connection.

Today is about syncing your rhythm with another ~ not through words or action, but through *breath*. Through simply *being with*.

The archetype of the day is The Breath Weaver ~ the part of you that senses connection not by effort, but through embodied presence and nervous system trust.

Today's Symbols::

- Two pillows close but not touching, both indented by presence
- Lepidolite, for nervous system soothing, harmony, and co-regulation
- The Four of Swords, sacred rest, recovery, and wordless union
- A pair of whales swimming side by side, submerged in breath and silence

Reflection Prompts:

- When do I feel most connected to others ~ and is it always through conversation or touch?
- How do I respond to stillness in relationships ~ with comfort, or anxiety?

- What might happen if I let breath be the bridge, instead of effort?

Integration Practice: Shared Breath Ritual

With a partner:

- Sit or lie facing each other, eyes closed or gently soft.
- Match your breathing ~ not perfectly, just *attuned*.
- Inhale together. Exhale slowly. No words.
- Do this for 3–5 minutes, holding hands or not.

Alone:

- Sit or lie down. Place your hands over your chest and belly.
- Whisper:

"I breathe with the rhythm of life. I am already in connection."

Let this practice remind you: Sometimes, shared presence is deeper than any exchange.

Closing Mantra for the Today ~

"I do not need to speak to be known. I breathe, and I belong. Intimacy lives in presence."

May 7 – The Day of Soulful Surrender

A story of trust, sacred letting go, and the transformative intimacy that begins when you stop holding back

There once was a soul who had learned to stay in control ~ especially in love.

They gave carefully. Received cautiously. Even in moments of closeness, something in them stayed slightly withdrawn ~ just enough to remain safe.

Desire was there. Affection, yes. But surrender? That required trust they weren't sure they had earned yet.

Then one quiet evening ~ as the Northern sky draped itself in velvet blue, or the Southern breeze moved softly through falling leaves ~ the soul's partner reached for them with complete presence.

No demands. No performance. Just an open hand, an open gaze.

And something in the soul shifted ~ not with drama, but with permission.

They softened. They let go of how they looked. They let go of how they were supposed to sound, move, perform.

They didn't offer perfection. They offered *truth*.

"This is what I want. This is how I ache. This is where I need."

And in that surrender ~ not just of body, but of control ~ they felt themselves held in a way they had never known.

Not taken. *Received*.

May 7 carries the energy of 7, a number of deep trust, spiritual openness, and inward courage.

Today isn't about submitting. It's about soulful surrender ~ the willingness to let go of what guards you from the intimacy you actually crave.

The archetype of the day is The Sacred Opener ~ the part of you that knows strength isn't only in holding it together, but in *melting where it's safe to do so.*

Today's Symbols::

- A loosely knotted ribbon slowly unwinding, soft and graceful
- Moonstone, for inner trust, emotional surrender, and fluid vulnerability
- The The Hanged One (Hanged Man), surrendering old perspectives, softening into truth
- A river meeting the sea, not losing itself ~ but becoming something more

Reflection Prompts:

- What part of myself have I kept guarded, even in the presence of love?
- What fear does surrender awaken in me ~ and where did that fear begin?
- Who, or what, might be worthy of seeing me without my armor?

Integration Practice: Sacred Letting Go

With a partner:

- Create a space of slowness.
- Share one truth you've held back ~ something tender, something you want, or something you're afraid to say.
- Then invite your partner to do the same.

Don't fix. Just hold.

Alone:

- Write the sentence:

"I am allowed to surrender when…"

- Finish it multiple times.
- Then lie down, breathe deeply, and place your hands on your lower belly. Whisper:

"I am safe to soften. I am held ~ even here."

Closing Mantra for the Today ~

"Surrender is not weakness. It is the sacred act of trusting love enough to open. I release control. I receive connection."

May 8 – The Day of Inner Devotion

A story of sacred commitment, embodied care, and the quiet intimacy that deepens when you return to love ~ not because you have to, but because you choose to

There once was a soul who thought devotion meant staying.

Staying in the room. Staying in the routine. Staying committed no matter the cost.

But over time, staying became surviving ~ not choosing.

The spark dulled. The intimacy faded into logistics. They shared beds, calendars, maybe even laughter ~ but something sacred had gone silent.

Then one morning ~ as the Northern light shimmered through early blossoms, or the Southern shadows lengthened over quiet soil ~ the soul woke beside their partner… and *noticed* them.

Not out of obligation. But out of reverence.

The curve of their back. The rhythm of their breath. The way they stirred slightly as light moved across the sheets.

The soul touched their arm ~ not to wake them, not to ask for anything ~ but as a return.

A wordless vow: *I choose this. I choose you.*

"Devotion," the soul realized, "is not about staying where love once was. It's about *revisiting love daily* ~ with presence."

May 8 carries the energy of 8, the number of enduring strength, conscious commitment, and balanced intimacy.

Today asks not, *"Do I love?"* But:

"How do I show up for love ~ especially when no one is watching?"

The archetype of the day is The Soul Devotee ~ the self who doesn't confuse habit with care, but who chooses love in motion, again and again, through presence, attention, and quiet touch.

Today's Symbols::

- A cup of tea placed gently on a shared bedside table, still steaming
- Ruby, for commitment, heart-fire, and passion that endures with grace
- A pair of cranes nesting together, heads bowed in mirror stillness

Reflection Prompts:

- Where have I confused devotion with duty ~ and what's the difference?

- How do I show up for love when no one is asking for it?
- What would devotion feel like if it were rooted in choice, not pressure?

Integration Practice: Small Act of Sacred Return

With a partner:

- Today, do one small thing that shows love with no expectation ~ a gesture, a message, a gentle touch.
- Do it not for romance, but for *presence*.
- And if the moment allows, whisper:

"I still choose this."

Alone:

- Place your hand on your chest. Breathe slowly.
- Write or whisper:

"Here's what I'm devoted to ~ in love, in touch, in truth."

- Then light a candle for that devotion ~ even if it's just to your own unfolding.

Closing Mantra for the Today ~

"My love is a living choice. I return, not out of habit ~ but out of reverence. This is my devotion ~ quiet, real, and enough."

May 9 – The Day of Healing Desire

A story of reclaimed longing, embodied permission, and remembering that desire is not a danger ~ it's a doorway to deeper connection

There once was a soul who had been taught to fear their desire.

To keep it quiet. To tone it down. To give, but never need. To be wanted ~ but not to *want*.

Over time, their sensuality became fragmented. They craved connection, but couldn't name what they needed. They felt pleasure, but didn't feel safe in it.

Then one night ~ as the Northern air thickened with scent, or the Southern winds quieted to a hush ~ the soul lay beside their partner, heart aching with unsaid longing.

And instead of pushing it down, they said:

"There's something I want ~ and I'm scared to ask for it."

They didn't make it sound perfect. They didn't wrap it in humor or apology.

They just let themselves *feel* it ~ fully.

Their partner didn't rush in. They listened. They nodded. And then ~ they met them there, with care.

And in that moment, the soul realized:

"Desire isn't dangerous. What's dangerous is silencing the truth of my body."

May 9 carries the energy of 9, the number of emotional culmination, release, and soulful honesty.

Today invites you into a healing of desire ~ not to indulge recklessly, but to *reclaim what has always been yours.*

Desire that is safe. Desire that is heard. Desire that honors both *you* and the *other.*

The archetype of the day is The Reclaimer ~ the self who steps back into sensual truth, emotional longing, and embodied requests ~ without shame.

Today's Symbols::

- A velvet ribbon slowly unfurling on bare skin, sensual and soft
- Carnelian, for igniting safe passion, inner permission, and creative fire
- The Queen of Cups, emotionally rich, intuitive, and open in truth
- A lioness lying down with her eyes open, strong in want, but calm in expression

Reflection Prompts:

- What have I longed for ~ in touch, closeness, or emotional presence ~ but have struggled to name?
- Where did I learn that desire made me unsafe or unworthy?
- What would it mean to speak one of those longings ~ and let it be heard with love?

Integration Practice: Write the Unspoken Want

With a partner:

- Write down one thing you desire ~ emotionally, physically, spiritually.
- Swap notes and read without judgment. Then say:

"Thank you for trusting me."

- Whether it's acted on or simply witnessed, this is healing.

Alone:

- Write a letter that begins:

"Dear body, I want to feel…"

- Let the truth come ~ gently, messily, raw.
- End it with:

"I give myself permission to want."

¶
¶
¶
¶
¶
¶
¶
¶
¶
¶
¶
¶
¶

Closing Mantra for the Today ~

"Desire is not a danger ~ it is a language. I honor what I long for. I speak it with courage, and I receive it with care."

May 10 – The Day of Sacred Touch

A story of healing fingertips, intuitive connection, and remembering that touch is not only sensual ~ it is spiritual

There once was a soul who had been touched many times ~ but rarely *felt*.

They had known hands that reached in passion. Hands that rushed. Hands that took before asking.

Over time, their body became a place of performance, not presence.

But then one evening ~ as the Northern sky burned low with spring fire, or the Southern land quieted under warm dusk ~ they rested beside their partner in stillness.

And something changed.

No urgency. No aim. Just a single hand placed over their heart ~ still, warm, *aware*.

It didn't move. It didn't press.

It simply stayed.

And in that staying, something old and scared inside the soul… exhaled.

"This," they realized, "is what it feels like to be touched with reverence."

Not for pleasure alone. Not for taking.

But to be *met* ~ gently, wholly, and without expectation.

May 10 carries the energy of 1 (1 + 0), the number of initiation, soulful beginning, and body-rooted truth.

Today calls you back to sacred touch ~ the kind that doesn't rush to arouse, but *awakens what is sacred* in the moment.

The archetype of the day is The Sacred Sensor ~ the self who knows touch is not a transaction, but a language, a ceremony, a healing bridge.

Today's Symbols::

- A pair of hands resting on bare skin, unmoving but deeply attuned
- Rhodonite, for touch-based healing, heart activation, and safe sensuality
- The Ace of Cups, the beginning of emotional embodiment and gentle offering
- A hummingbird hovering above a flower, near but never forceful

Reflection Prompts:
- When was the last time I felt truly safe in someone's touch ~ not because it was perfect, but because it was present?
- How do I want to be touched ~ emotionally, spiritually, physically ~ and have I ever named that?
- What would it mean to offer touch as a form of listening ~ not action?

Integration Practice: Sacred Hands Ritual

With a partner:
- Sit or lie together in stillness.
- Each take turns placing your hands on the other's body ~ heart, back, hips ~ with full attention and no movement.
- Breathe.
- Say aloud:

"My touch honors you. There is nothing you need to give back."

Alone:
- Rub your hands together gently until warm.
- Place one over your heart, the other on your lower abdomen.
- Whisper:

"This body is sacred. This skin is safe."

Remain for 5 minutes, eyes closed. Let the stillness be your ceremony.

Closing Mantra for the Today ~

"I touch with reverence. I receive without fear. In this moment, my body is not a performance ~ it is a prayer."

May 11 – The Day of Union and Release

A story of shared depth, cyclical passion, and the soul's wisdom to both merge and let go ~ without fear of loss

There once was a soul who believed intimacy had to last forever.

That once connected, two must stay fused ~ Every moment shared. Every breath in sync. Every desire matched.

They feared that separation meant rejection. That rest meant withdrawal. That change in rhythm meant love was dying.

But one evening ~ as the Northern moon waxed full above awakening branches, or the Southern winds curled into the cooling dark ~ the soul and their partner lay side by side after deep closeness.

Still naked. Still present. But apart ~ by choice, not rejection.

There was no talking. No rush to return to holding.

Just space. And breath. And the deep knowing that connection didn't need *constant confirmation*.

"We are not one," the soul whispered, "but we have touched what is shared ~ and that is enough."

In that moment, they understood: Real union is not just merging ~ it's also releasing, with love.

May 11 carries the energy of 2 (1 + 1), the number of relationship, reflection, and emotional balance.

Today reminds you: Union and release are not opposites. They are sacred partners ~ a rhythm that allows true intimacy to breathe.

The archetype of the day is The Harmonized Lover ~ the self who meets in depth without clinging, who can both open fully *and* honor the need to rest, to separate, to self-return.

Today's Symbols::

- A full moon reflected in water, not touching it, yet entirely present
- Labradorite, for emotional transitions, psychic clarity, and energetic boundaries
- The Two of Swords, peaceful decision, reflective connection, duality in harmony
- Two wolves on opposite ridges, howling in echo ~ not to possess, but to call and be heard

Reflection Prompts:

- Do I equate closeness with permanence ~ and distance with rejection?

- How can I honor both union and space as sacred aspects of intimacy?
- What might shift if I saw release as love, not loss?

Integration Practice: Merge and Separate

With a partner:

- After sharing closeness ~ whether touch, conversation, or lovemaking ~ intentionally separate for a few minutes.
- Sit in silence. Journal. Walk alone.
- Then come back together, gently.

Say aloud:

"We are not one. But we are together. This space honors our return."

Alone:

- Reflect on a moment of connection that ended naturally ~ a relationship, a season, a moment of pleasure.
- Write:

"I release the need to hold what has already been complete. I honor what was shared."

Let this become your rhythm: merge, breathe, release, *remember.*

Closing Mantra for the Today ~

"I love without clutching. I connect without fear. I release without losing what was real."

May 12 – The Day of Intimate Trust

A story of emotional safety, embodied confidence, and the kind of touch, truth, and tenderness that grows only where trust has been nurtured

There once was a soul who had learned to offer parts of themselves carefully ~ like petals, one at a time.

Not because they didn't long for closeness, but because they had once given everything too fast... and been left.

They learned to hold back. To measure. To wait for proof that the ground was safe.

Then one tender afternoon ~ as the Northern light danced through branches, or the Southern chill wrapped the earth in stillness ~ the soul rested in their partner's arms after sharing something deeply vulnerable.

A story. A fear. A trembling truth.

Their partner didn't rush to fix. They didn't interrupt with affirmation. They simply... *stayed.*

And in that presence, the soul's guard dropped ~ not as surrender, but as relief.

"Trust," the soul thought, "is not built in the big promises. It's built in the still moments after I let myself be seen… and no one turns away."

May 12 holds the energy of 3 (1 + 2), the number of expression, soul-to-soul communication, and emotional reciprocity.

Today is a day to honor intimate trust ~ not just with others, but with yourself: to trust what you feel, what you need, and what your body whispers when it's safe.

The archetype of the day is The Inner Witness ~ the self who trusts not because everything is perfect, but because presence has proven to be enough.

Today's Symbols::

- A white cloth folded beside a love letter, untouched and intentional
- Pink opal, for emotional healing, softness, and the rebuilding of relational trust
- The Six of Cups, tender memory, inner child comfort, and nostalgic safety
- A dove landing near open palms, unstartled, choosing to stay

Reflection Prompts:

- Where in my life am I learning to trust again ~ not in words, but in actions?
- What moment of tenderness helped restore a part of me I thought was lost?
- Do I trust myself to speak my needs? And can I hold the silence that follows, without shrinking?

Integration Practice: The Stay Moment

With a partner:

- Share one story or truth that feels vulnerable ~ it can be simple or deep.
- Ask your partner to simply listen ~ no comments, no comfort, just presence.
- Afterward, hold hands or breathe together in silence for at least 2 minutes.

Alone:

- Write about a time when someone stayed ~ emotionally, physically, spiritually.
- Reflect:

"What did that teach me about trust?"
Then whisper: *"I am safe to share. I am safe to stay."*

Closing Mantra for the Today ~

"I offer myself where presence lives. I trust not the promise, but the pause. Intimacy grows where I am seen and still safe."

May 13 – The Day of Sensual Receiving

A story of embodied pleasure, softened receptivity, and remembering that to truly receive is an act of sacred power

There once was a soul who was always giving.

They offered comfort, closeness, affection ~ without hesitation, without limit.

But when love was offered to them ~ through gifts, through words, through *touch* ~ they flinched.

Not visibly. But inwardly, they questioned:

"Do I deserve this?" "Have I earned this?" "What must I give back in return?"

Then one slow evening ~ as the Northern sky turned lavender in the deep exhale of day, or the Southern leaves fell with ceremonial hush ~ their partner reached for them.

No expectation. Just a hand on the thigh. A kiss on the collarbone. A breath.

And the soul felt a flicker ~ not of desire, but of *tension*.

They were afraid to let go… to be touched without performing.

But they breathed. And they stayed. And for the first time in a long time, they let themselves receive.

No giving back. No owing. Just opening.

"Receiving," the soul realized, "isn't passive. It's devotional."

May 13 carries the energy of 4 (1 + 3), the number of embodiment, grounded love, and sustainable intimacy.

Today asks you to practice sensual receiving ~ to let yourself be the one who melts, opens, softens… without needing to reciprocate immediately.

The archetype of the day is The Open Vessel ~ the self who understands that to receive touch, care, and pleasure with presence is an act of power, not weakness.

Today's Symbols::

- A bowl being filled drop by drop, never overflowing, just accepting
- Peach moonstone, for feminine receptivity, sensual attunement, and divine balance
- The Queen of Pentacles, grounded, nurturing, abundant in receiving and care
- A cat curled in sunlight, warm, slow, completely surrendered to pleasure

Reflection Prompts:

— Where in my life do I resist receiving ~ and why?
— Do I associate being touched or cherished with obligation or performance?
— What would it feel like to receive with no fear of owing anything in return?

Integration Practice: The Receiving Ritual

With a partner:

— Let them touch you slowly, for no purpose other than comfort, presence, or pleasure.
— No need to respond. Just breathe and receive.
— Afterward, place your hand on their heart and say:

"Thank you. I let myself receive."

Alone:

— Lie down in a quiet space.
— Place lotion or oil on your hands and slowly anoint your own body ~ arms, legs, belly, chest.
— Say aloud:

"I receive myself. I soften into this body."

This is how we practice worthiness ~ through touch, without tension.

Closing Mantra for the Today ~

"I do not need to give to be worthy of love. I receive with presence. I open without apology."

May 14 – The Day of Soul-Made Sex

A story of embodied union, sacred pleasure, and the kind of connection where every breath, every movement, becomes a prayer between two souls

There once was a soul who had known sex as a performance.

They had learned the choreography ~ what to say, when to move, how to please.

They had chased intensity, checked for approval, played every part.

But deep inside, they longed for something else: Not just *closeness* ~ but *communion*. Not just *pleasure* ~ but *presence*.

Then one night ~ as the Northern winds whispered through budding trees, or the Southern stars blanketed the cooling sky ~ the soul made love without armor.

They weren't trying to impress. They weren't trying to disappear.

They were *inside themselves* ~ body, breath, and soul.

Their partner met them there ~ Not to lead or follow, but to move as one: slow, intuitive, reverent.

Each touch was a word. Each breath a response. Each gaze a *devotion*.

"This isn't sex," the soul thought. "This is a conversation between souls ~ and every part of me is finally speaking."

May 14 carries the energy of 5 (1 + 4), the number of movement, expression, and sacred liberation.

Today invites you to explore soul-made sex ~ intimacy that is not driven by urgency, but by *attunement*. Not fueled by fantasy, but by *presence*.

The archetype of the day is The Soulful Lover ~ the self who brings their entire being into union: mind, body, emotion, and spirit ~ and honors it all as sacred.

Today's Symbols::

- Two figures entwined in candlelight, foreheads touching, eyes closed
- Red jasper, for grounding erotic energy, spiritual strength, and root chakra safety
- The Lovers card, as soulful fusion ~ not decision, but devotion
- A swan pair in water, circling one another slowly in mirrored motion

Reflection Prompts:

- What does "sacred sex" mean to me ~ and have I ever truly felt it?
- What part of myself wants to be seen ~ not just in the act, but in the stillness before and after?
- What would it feel like to make love without leaving my own body behind?

Integration Practice: A Soulful Union Ritual

With a partner:

- Create space for slow, intentional closeness ~ candles, silence, soft lighting.
- Before any physical touch, sit face-to-face. Hold eye contact. Breathe together.
- Speak one truth aloud:

"Here is what I want to give…" "Here is what I long to feel…"

Then let the body become a vessel of truth, not performance.

Alone:

- Light a candle. Touch yourself not to release, but to honor.
- Whisper:

"This is sacred. I am whole. I meet myself in presence."

This is not just sex. It is soul work ~ through skin, sensation, surrender.

Closing Mantra for the Today ~

"My body is not separate from my soul. I make love with presence. I touch and am touched as a sacred act of becoming."

May 15 – The Day of Loving Integration

A story of wholeness, post-intimacy tenderness, and the soul's ability to hold pleasure, vulnerability, and truth in the same breath

There once was a soul who had known the high of closeness ~ and the low that often followed.

They had experienced passionate nights followed by morning silence. Words spoken in heat, forgotten in daylight. Touches that felt real in the moment, but left them questioning afterward.

They began to believe that intimacy was temporary ~ a brief escape from loneliness, not a lasting return to self.

But one golden morning ~ as the Northern light spilled across tangled sheets, or the Southern quiet deepened into early twilight ~ the soul and their partner lay quietly, breath synced, bodies still humming from the night before.

There was no need to speak.

The soul felt full. Not just satisfied, but *integrated*.

All of them ~ the vulnerable parts, the passionate parts, the scared and sacred ~ felt held.

"This," the soul realized, "is what love feels like when it doesn't disappear after desire. It lingers. It integrates. It *stays*."

May 15 holds the energy of 6 (1 + 5), the number of emotional equilibrium, healing, and the weaving together of experience into truth.

Today is about integration after intimacy ~ the ability to hold the aftermath of closeness with tenderness, not avoidance.

The archetype of the day is The Wholehearted Soul ~ the self who no longer splits between passion and presence, but who brings all parts of themselves into love and lives *in the afterglow with grace*.

Today's Symbols::

- A blanket draped across two intertwined hands, soft, unforced, warm
- Smoky quartz, for grounding, clarity, and post-experience embodiment
- The Temperance card, soulful alchemy, emotional balance, sacred blending
- A koala nestled in eucalyptus, still and settled after deep connection

Reflection Prompts:

- What happens to me after intimacy ~ emotionally, spiritually, physically?
- Do I feel closer, or do I retreat? And why?
- How can I carry love through the aftermath ~ in small gestures, inner calm, or shared stillness?

Integration Practice: The After Ritual

With a partner:

- After intimacy, remain close ~ no rush to dress, no retreat into activity.
- Light a candle. Breathe together. Share three words each that describe how you feel.
- Hold one another and say aloud: *"I'm still with you."*

Alone:

- Sit with your hand on your heart.
- Write the sentence:
- *"After love, I feel…"*
- Let the truth come, even if it's messy.
- Then say:

"All of me belongs here."

Integration is where love becomes real.

¶

¶

¶

¶

¶

¶

¶

¶

¶

¶

¶

Closing Mantra for the Today ~

"I do not leave myself after love. I carry the softness, the spark, the truth ~ into the next breath. I am whole in intimacy, and whole afterward."

May 16 – The Day of Emotional Communion

A story of soul-deep resonance, unspoken connection, and the intimacy that transcends touch when two hearts meet in presence

There once was a soul who had mastered physical closeness ~ but longed for something rarer: emotional union.

They had kissed with passion. Shared beds. Even said, "I love you" with conviction.

But often, their heart still felt like it was speaking into a void.

Until one quiet evening ~ as the Northern trees rustled with blooming promise, or the Southern air stilled under a softening sky ~ the soul sat in silence with their partner.

No touching. No talking. Just eyes… meeting.

In that stillness, something ancient stirred.

There was no need to explain the grief they were carrying, no need to narrate the ache behind their smile.

It was understood.

And their partner ~ seeing it all ~ simply nodded.

Not with words, but with *presence*.

"This," the soul thought, "is communion. Not just connection. Not just closeness. Communion ~ where my soul is held, not handled."

May 16 carries the energy of 7 (1 + 6), the number of spiritual attunement, emotional honesty, and intuitive knowing.

Today calls you into emotional communion ~ the kind of intimacy that needs no translation, because it arises from deep listening and a willingness to *be with*.

The archetype of the day is The Silent Witness ~ the self who doesn't need to fix, touch, or even speak ~ only to be fully, wholly *present*.

Today's Symbols::

- Two figures sitting back-to-back, eyes closed, breathing in tandem
- Celestite, for gentle communication, inner clarity, and emotional resonance
- The High Priestess, keeper of depth, intuition, and sacred silence
- A white deer emerging from mist, noticed, not startled

Reflection Prompts:

- Have I experienced emotional communion ~ and if so, how did I know it was real?
- Do I listen to connect, or to solve? Do I speak to be known, or to protect?
- What would it feel like to be emotionally met, without words?

Integration Practice: Eye Gazing & Heart Listening

With a partner:

- Sit facing each other. Eyes open. Hands over your own hearts.
- Gaze silently for 3–5 minutes. No words, no movement.
- Afterward, share only this:

"Here's what I felt when I looked into you..."

Alone:

- Sit before a mirror or with your journal.
- Place your hand on your chest and ask:

"What truth have I been waiting for someone to feel in me?"

- Write or whisper that truth aloud.

Let the act of emotional witnessing become your communion.

Closing Mantra for the Today ~

"I am not alone in my depth. I am seen in silence. I trust that emotional communion needs no explanation ~ only presence."

May 17 – The Day of Sacred Slowness

A story of unrushed intimacy, reverent pacing, and the truth that what is most sacred often arrives only when we stop hurrying it

There once was a soul who had only known intimacy in speed.

Quick kisses. Fast passion. Conversations squeezed between tasks.

Even in connection, there was always a clock ticking in the background ~ as if love had to be *efficient* to be real.

Then one evening ~ as the Northern sky blushed in slow twilight, or the Southern winds hummed low through golden trees ~ the soul and their partner moved differently.

Slower. Softer. No script.

Each button undone was a pause. Each breath an invitation. There was no rush to climax, no race to closeness ~ only presence.

And somewhere in that still unfolding, the soul felt something they hadn't before:

"Time dissolved. And in its place... sacredness appeared."

Not in the act, but in the ritual of arrival.

May 17 holds the energy of 8 (1 + 7), the number of soulful strength, balance, and sustained connection.

Today is an invitation into sacred slowness ~ not laziness, not delay, but the kind of slowing that brings you into full presence with pleasure, emotion, and spirit.

The archetype of the day is The Slow Lover ~ the self who understands that what's truly intimate can't be hurried, and that slowness is not resistance ~ it's reverence.

Today's Symbols::

- A single droplet falling into a bowl, rippling outward in quiet grace
- Blue calcite, for calm touch, soft expression, and soul-deep relaxation
- The Knight of Pentacles, steady, devoted, honoring each step with care
- A tortoise resting in sunlight, every movement sacred, unshaken

Reflection Prompts:

- Where in my life am I rushing what wants to unfold slowly ~ love, pleasure, healing?

- What do I fear will happen if I slow down? What might I finally feel?
- Can I honor intimacy not as a destination ~ but as a moment-by-moment presence?

Integration Practice: Touch in Time

With a partner:

- Make an agreement to move slowly. No goal. No endpoint.
- Use just your fingertips ~ tracing arms, neck, back.
- Set a timer if helpful. Five minutes of touch in silence.
- Breathe together. Whisper nothing. Let time stretch.

Alone:

- Touch your own body with the same intention.
- Move slowly, with reverence ~ not to stimulate, but to sense.
- Say softly:

"This body is not in a hurry. This touch is my return."

Closing Mantra for the Today ~

"I move with devotion. I love in rhythm. In slowness, I meet what is truly sacred."

May 18 – The Day of Tender Power

A story of gentle strength, soul-led intimacy, and the truth that being soft in love is not weakness ~ it is the deepest kind of courage

There once was a soul who had always been the strong one.

They protected. Provided. Performed.

They held space for others. They were dependable, composed ~ even during intimacy, even when inside they were craving to fall into someone's arms and simply… *be held*.

But vulnerability felt like surrender. And surrender felt like risk.

Then one evening ~ as the Northern winds stilled under a canopy of quiet stars, or the Southern earth curled into mist and mulch and dusk ~ the soul exhaled in their partner's arms.

Not dramatically. Not as collapse.

But as *permission*.

A single tear. A word spoken too slowly. A body that trembled ~ not from fear, but from finally being safe enough to *not be in control*.

Their partner didn't try to fix it. They stayed. And the soul discovered something new:

"This is strength, too ~ the kind that doesn't grip... but *opens*."

May 18 carries the energy of 9 (1 + 8), the number of culmination, healing, and embodied truth.

Today asks you to explore your tender power ~ the kind of strength that allows tears, trust, and *touch* to coexist in the same breath.

The archetype of the day is The Courageous Heart ~ the self who no longer confuses armor with strength, and who knows that the bravest thing they can do... is soften in the presence of love.

Today's Symbols::

— A rose blooming between two stones, soft but unbroken
— Rhodochrosite, for heart healing, emotional release, and loving the inner child
— The Strength card, not force ~ but patient, loving confidence
— A horse lowering its head to a small child's hand, regal and gentle

Reflection Prompts:

— Where have I been told that strength means withholding ~ and do I still believe it?

- What would it feel like to let someone see me shake, cry, or ask for comfort ~ and stay?
- Can I hold my tenderness as power, not proof of fragility?

Integration Practice: Let Someone In

With a partner:

- Name one thing you're carrying that feels heavy or vulnerable ~ even just a phrase:

"This week has been hard." "I don't always know how to ask for softness."

- Then ask:

"Can you just hold me, no words?"

Alone:

- Place both hands over your heart.
- Speak aloud:

"My softness is strong. My need is holy."

- Write one sentence to yourself that you would want to hear from someone who truly sees your strength and your ache.

¶
¶
¶
¶
¶
¶
¶
¶
¶

Closing Mantra for the Today ~

"I do not lose power when I open. I become whole. My tenderness is my courage."

May 19 – The Day of Sacred Boundaries in Love

A story of self-honoring, relational truth, and the deep intimacy that becomes possible when you stop abandoning yourself to be close

There once was a soul who gave everything in love ~ except space.

They said yes to things that hurt. They stayed when their body whispered "no." They mistook closeness for surrender, sacrifice for commitment.

For a while, it worked. Or seemed to.

But beneath the surface, they grew tired. Touch no longer felt nourishing. Presence began to feel like pressure.

Then one evening ~ as the Northern sky blushed in late spring fire, or the Southern winds circled dry leaves in farewell ~ the soul paused before intimacy.

And said softly:

"I need to stop here." "I need to be close, *without crossing myself*."

Their partner didn't flinch. They nodded. Held space.

And the soul realized something sacred:

"Boundaries don't keep love out. They *shape* love into something I can stay inside."

May 19 carries the energy of 1 (1 + 9 = 10 → 1), the number of initiation, identity, and empowered self-claiming.

Today is not about pulling away. It's about staying whole while staying close.

The archetype of the day is The Inner Gatekeeper ~ the part of you that doesn't build walls, but *welcomes wisely*. That honors your yes, your no, and your sacred *maybe later*.

Today's Symbols::

- A door slightly ajar with warm light beyond, and a hand resting gently on the frame
- Black tourmaline, for energetic protection and grounded self-trust
- The Seven of Wands, holding firm not from fear ~ but from self-respect
- A deer in tall grass, alert yet calm, choosing when to step forward

Reflection Prompts:

- Where in intimacy have I said yes when my truth was no ~ or not yet?
- What boundary might deepen my connection ~ rather than disrupt it?
- How can I ask for space or pacing in a way that honors both me and the one I love?

Integration Practice: Sacred Self-Check

With a partner:

- Before physical or emotional closeness, ask yourself:

"What part of me needs to be named right now?"

- Share it aloud ~ even just one sentence.

"I'm feeling tender and I need to go slower." "I want to be close, but I also want to stay in my own breath."

Alone:

- Write down three boundaries that support your wholeness in connection.

"I can pause in intimacy without guilt." "I can speak my discomfort without apology." "I can love and still leave space for myself."

— Post them where you can revisit them when the pull to abandon yourself returns.

Closing Mantra for the Today ~

"I protect what is sacred in me. I stay whole in love. Boundaries do not push love away ~ they give it shape."

May 20 – The Day of Reverent Closeness

A story of sacred nearness, soul-filled presence, and the intimacy that deepens when we stop touching out of habit ~ and start touching with devotion

There once was a soul who had become accustomed to closeness ~ but had forgotten to feel it.

They kissed goodbye while thinking of errands. They held hands during movies but not during silence. They touched often, but rarely with reverence.

Their body had become familiar. So had their partner's. And familiarity, while comforting, had made something sacred feel... routine.

Then one evening ~ as the Northern dusk stretched golden across soft fields, or the Southern air turned cool and fragrant before nightfall ~ the soul watched their partner undress slowly, not for seduction, but for sleep.

And in that ordinary moment, something extraordinary happened.

They saw them ~ fully. The curve of a shoulder. The breath in the ribcage. The way they folded the blanket like a ritual.

It wasn't erotic. It was *holy*.

They walked over, wrapped their arms around their partner's back, and said softly:

"I want to be close to you ~ not just with my body, but with my whole self."

May 20 carries the energy of 2 (2 + 0), the number of reflection, emotional attunement, and relational presence.

Today is an invitation into reverent closeness ~ the kind that feels less like reaching out and more like *returning home*.

The archetype of the day is The Devotional Partner ~ the self who shows up in quiet gestures, soft words, and embodied love ~ not to perform, but to *honor*.

Today's Symbols::

- Two hands cradling a single cup, careful and steady
- Rose quartz, for gentle love, heart-centered presence, and unconditional softness
- The Ten of Cups, fullness in connection, everyday magic in love
- A fox resting against another, still, close, completely at ease

Reflection Prompts:

- Where in my relationship(s) have I gone through the motions ~ without full presence?
- What happens when I approach nearness not as routine, but as ritual?
- What small gesture today can I give or receive with reverence?

Integration Practice: Touch with Intention

With a partner:

- Choose one physical interaction today ~ holding hands, hugging, laying beside one another ~ and perform it slowly, with awareness.
- Before or after, say:

"This closeness matters to me. I'm here ~ fully."

Alone:

- Place your hand on your heart or cheek.
- Whisper:

"This is how I will hold myself ~ gently, again and again."

Let your body remember: Closeness is not a given. It is a gift.

Closing Mantra for the Today ~

"I do not rush through connection. I meet it with care, with breath, with devotion. Love is sacred ~ even in stillness."

May 21 – The Day of Magnetic Honesty

A story of raw truth, soul-level attraction, and the intimacy that deepens not in perfection ~ but in the courage to be fully, undeniably real

There once was a soul who thought they had to be likable to be loved.

They measured every word. Softened their edges. Shared only what wouldn't shake the ground between them.

They became fluent in emotional editing.

But after a while, even their lover couldn't find them anymore. Not the full them ~ just the polished version, the digestible one.

Then one evening ~ as the Northern breeze carried the scent of early summer, or the Southern air grew still with changing season ~ the soul sat across from their partner and, for once, didn't clean it up.

They said the messy thing. The vulnerable thing. The truth that had teeth and tenderness in equal measure.

And their partner didn't leave. They leaned in.

Closer. Softer. More *attracted* ~ not in spite of the honesty, but *because* of it.

"This," the soul whispered inside, "is what it feels like to be loved for who I am ~ not who I pretend to be."

May 21 carries the energy of 3 (2 + 1), the number of expression, soul voice, and embodied truth.

Today is about magnetic honesty ~ the kind of truth that may tremble when it's spoken, but draws others closer instead of pushing them away.

The archetype of the day is The Unfiltered Flame ~ the self who speaks from the heart, not to provoke, but to *liberate*, and who trusts that real intimacy begins when masks come off.

Today's Symbols::

— A match igniting softly in the dark, both light and heat
— Amazonite, for courageous communication, emotional balance, and vulnerability
— The Page of Swords, truth spoken bravely, even before it's perfect
— A raven perched beside another, watching with intelligence and curiosity

Reflection Prompts:

— Where have I been editing my truth to stay safe in love?
— What am I afraid will happen if I say what I really feel, need, or believe?

- What if honesty is what magnetizes the connection I truly crave?

Integration Practice: Speak the Honest Sentence

With a partner:

- Take turns finishing the sentence:

"Something I haven't said out loud is…"

- Pause. Breathe.
- Let silence be the response before any fixing, advice, or explanation.

Alone:

- Write a letter to a past version of yourself who stayed silent in love.
- Begin:

"Here's what I wish I had said…"

- Let the words come through you unfiltered ~ this is your release.

Closing Mantra for the Today ~

"I speak from soul, not strategy. My honesty is not a risk ~ it is a magnet for truth. I am worthy of being loved in full."

May 22 – The Day of Sensory Union

A story of embodied presence, sacred attunement, and the kind of intimacy that unfolds not through words, but through every activated sense

There once was a soul who had always approached intimacy through thought.

They said the right things. Held space with care. Loved from the neck up ~ articulate, attentive, and careful.

But something in their body remained untouched. They gave affection, but rarely *sensed* it. They moved through love as an idea ~ not an experience.

Then one day ~ as the Northern world ripened with early summer scent, or the Southern winds carried dried leaves across worn stone ~ the soul paused.

Their partner kissed the back of their hand. No words. No suggestion. Just a moment of contact.

The scent of their skin. The brush of breath on their fingers. The warmth in their chest.

Suddenly, everything slowed.

They *felt* the kiss in their whole body ~ as if their senses were finally turned *on*.

"This," the soul thought, "is union. Not a thought ~ a sensation. A surrender into presence."

May 22 carries the energy of 4 (2 + 2), the number of grounding, body-centered connection, and sacred sensuality.

Today invites you to experience sensory union ~ not performance, not expectation, but shared attention through *touch, scent, sound, taste, and presence.*

The archetype of the day is The Embodied Listener ~ the self who connects through sensation, who knows intimacy is not just something we think or say ~ it's something we *feel, inhale, taste, and move through*.

Today's Symbols::

- A tray of herbs, oil, and linen, prepared without urgency
- Jasmine essential oil or sandalwood, for sensual awakening and grounding
- The Ace of Pentacles, a new beginning through tangible connection
- A cat rubbing its cheek against a palm, fully surrendered to sensory pleasure

Reflection Prompts:

- Which of my senses do I most associate with intimacy ~ and which have I ignored?
- Have I allowed myself to slow down enough to truly feel my partner ~ or myself?
- What sensory experiences make me feel the most grounded, alive, and connected?

Integration Practice: Five-Sense Intimacy

With a partner:

- Share a five-sense ritual together. Slowly. Attuned.

Ideas:

- Sight: Gaze for one full minute.
- Touch: Caress without destination.
- Scent: Light incense or use oil together.
- Sound: Play soft music or speak affirmations aloud.
- Taste: Feed each other a piece of fruit or chocolate ~ slowly.

Alone:

- Prepare a space for solo sensory immersion.
- Use scent, fabric, warmth, and soothing sounds.
- Say aloud:

"I feel my body. I sense my life. I am here in fullness."

Let this become your sensory prayer.

Closing Mantra for the Today ~

"I open to intimacy through presence. I meet my beloved with every sense awake. I am here ~ in body, in breath, in truth."

May 23 – The Day of Erotic Self-Trust

A story of embodied confidence, sensual autonomy, and reclaiming desire not as something given to you ~ but something that rises from within

There once was a soul who thought desire had to be earned.

They waited to be wanted. To be touched first. To be told they were worthy before they could feel their own heat.

They believed erotic energy belonged to someone else ~ something awakened by another, not something that already lived inside them.

Then one night ~ as the Northern moon arched high in an indigo sky, or the Southern mist brushed low across cooling fields ~ they lit a candle, stood in front of the mirror, and placed one hand on their belly.

And in the stillness, they didn't look for flaws. They didn't wait to be seen.

They *saw themselves.*

And more than that ~ they *trusted* what they felt in their own skin. The heat. The ache. The pulse of power that said:

"I don't need permission to feel alive. I already belong to this body. This body is mine ~ and it is enough."

May 23 holds the energy of 5 (2 + 3), the number of liberation, embodied energy, and creative expression through passion.

Today calls you to embrace erotic self-trust ~ not just knowing what you want, but *honoring that you're allowed to want it*.

The archetype of the day is The Inner Flame ~ the self who no longer waits to be chosen, but chooses themselves ~ through movement, pleasure, and raw, rooted presence.

Today's Symbols::

- A mirror reflecting candlelight over skin, soft and flickering
- Carnelian, for boldness, sexual confidence, and creative embodiment
- The Queen of Wands, magnetic, unapologetically sensual, and self-possessed
- A panther stretching at dusk, graceful and fully in command of its power

Reflection Prompts:

- Have I ever claimed my own desire ~ without apology or performance?

- Where do I still ask for permission to feel, want, or burn?
- What would it mean to trust my erotic self ~ not just in intimacy, but in life?

Integration Practice: Sensual Self-Recognition

Solo (or with a partner in witness only):

- Create a sacred space: candlelight, soft fabric, warm silence.
- Stand, sit, or lie down. Gently place your hands over your body ~ without expectation, only presence.
- Look in the mirror or close your eyes and say:

"I trust my body. I trust my desire. I am my own permission."

Optional: dance slowly, dress intentionally, or write a love letter to your own body.

With a partner:

- Instead of asking, "What do you want?"
- Ask: *"What does your body already know?"*
- Honor their answers ~ and share your own.

Closing Mantra for the Today ~

"I trust my heat. I honor my hunger. I am worthy of desire ~ not because it's given to me, but because it lives in me."

May 24 – The Day of Deep Listening in Love

A story of presence beyond words, emotional attunement, and the soul-level intimacy that grows when we stop waiting to speak ~ and start truly hearing

There once was a soul who had grown quiet in love ~ but not in peace.

They listened to keep harmony. They nodded, smiled, and agreed. But inside, they waited for someone to finally ask:

"And what about you?"

They had given so much space… and taken up so little.

Then one morning ~ as the Northern breeze shook petals loose from full spring bloom, or the Southern sky turned silver before a steady rain ~ the soul and their partner sat beside each other, a small distance between them.

And the partner asked a question ~ not casually, but slowly:

"Is there something I haven't heard you say yet?"

The soul didn't rush. They didn't know how to respond ~ not yet.

But they *felt it*. The openness. The safety. The readiness to receive.

And so, slowly, they began to speak ~ not perfectly, not fluently, but *truthfully*.

Their voice cracked. Their body trembled.

But their partner stayed silent... and present.

"This," the soul realized, "is what love sounds like when it listens."

May 24 carries the energy of 6 (2 + 4), the number of healing, receptivity, and emotional resonance.

Today invites you to practice deep listening in love ~ not just hearing the words, but receiving the *truth beneath them*.

The archetype of the day is The Attuned Partner ~ the self who listens not to respond or solve, but to understand and *hold space* for what longs to be voiced.

Today's Symbols::

- A clay bowl placed between two people, open and empty, ready to receive
- Blue kyanite, for open communication, heart-aligned expression, and mutual clarity
- The King of Cups, emotionally mature, deeply present, a listener of the unseen

- Two dolphins swimming parallel, close but not touching ~ in rhythm, in trust

Reflection Prompts:

- When was the last time I felt truly listened to ~ and what made it feel safe?
- What prevents me from listening deeply ~ to my partner, to myself?
- What am I ready to say, not to be fixed, but simply to be heard?

Integration Practice: Listening Without Interrupting

With a partner:

- Choose a quiet space. One speaks for 3 minutes without interruption.
- The other listens ~ not to reply, but to *feel*.
- Then switch roles.

Afterward, reflect:

"Here's what I heard…" "Here's what I felt when you said that…"

Alone:

- Write a letter from your heart to your mind:

"Here's what I've been trying to tell you…"

— Then sit in silence. Breathe. Listen inward.

Let this become your sacred listening space.

¶
¶
¶
¶
¶
¶
¶
¶
¶
¶
¶
¶

Closing Mantra for the Today ~

"I offer presence, not solutions. I hold space, not silence. Love listens first ~ then responds with care."

May 25 – The Day of Sacred Sensation

A story of awakened touch, sensual reverence, and the quiet knowing that the body is not just a vessel ~ it is a sanctuary of soul

There once was a soul who had lived from the shoulders up.

They thought. They planned. They gave, spoke, reasoned, even loved ~ all with careful thought.

But when it came to sensation ~ *feeling*, not analyzing ~ they often checked out.

Touch felt distant. Pleasure felt vague. Their body had become something they "used" rather than *lived in*.

Then one afternoon ~ as the Northern air warmed with the scent of early summer fruit, or the Southern shadows stretched long with late-autumn hush ~ the soul lay down and let themselves feel… just feel.

The breath on their skin. The way the sheet hugged their hip. The subtle pulse in their fingertips.

Nothing urgent. Nothing performed.

Just presence.

And suddenly, their body was no longer just flesh ~ it was a temple.

"This," they thought, "is sacred sensation ~ not for anyone else, but *for me*."

May 25 carries the energy of 7 (2 + 5), the number of spiritual depth, embodied wisdom, and conscious awareness.

Today invites you to experience your body not as an object ~ but as a *living altar* where sensation is sacred, not shameful.

The archetype of the day is The Sensory Mystic ~ the part of you who knows that the divine doesn't just live in the sky ~ it lives in *your skin, your breath*, and *your ability to feel*.

Today's Symbols::

- A body wrapped in silk, not for beauty ~ but for sensation
- Selenite, for energetic cleansing and attunement to subtle physical feeling
- The Ace of Cups, overflowing not with words, but with embodied emotion
- A sea otter floating alone, eyes closed, belly to the sun

Reflection Prompts:

- Do I allow myself to feel fully ~ or do I only permit sensation in certain moments?

- Where have I disconnected from my body, and what does that part need from me?
- What if every touch, every breath, every shiver was a spiritual experience?

Integration Practice: Touch Without Purpose

With a partner:

- Take 15 minutes to explore each other's bodies with no goal.
- Use fingertips, breath, maybe a feather or piece of cloth.
- Speak only if it deepens presence. Say:

"Tell me how this feels. Let me listen with my hands."

Alone:

- Run your fingers over your own body ~ slowly.
- Focus on temperature, texture, movement.
- Whisper:

"This is sacred. I am home in this body."

Let every inch be received with reverence.

Closing Mantra for the Today ~

"I awaken through sensation. My body is not separate from spirit. I honor each feeling as a form of remembering."

May 26 – The Day of Embodied Truth

A story of deep self-recognition, cellular honesty, and the moment when your body speaks what words never could ~ and you finally listen

There once was a soul who always tried to explain themselves.

They told their story. They shared their wounds. They offered carefully chosen words ~ all in the hope of being understood.

But still, something inside them remained unseen.

Because the truth they most needed to speak… wasn't verbal. It lived in their breath. In the tightness in their chest. In the way their hands trembled when they said, *"I'm fine."*

Then one day ~ as the Northern world grew lush with unstoppable bloom, or the Southern air quieted into the last hush of autumn ~ the soul laid down and wept.

No words. No reason.

Just their body telling the story their voice had silenced.

And for the first time, they didn't interrupt it. They didn't analyze it. They simply *let it move through*.

"This," they thought, "is truth ~ not spoken, but *embodied*. And I am strong enough now to let it live."

May 26 carries the energy of 8 (2 + 6), the number of inner authority, integration, and strength rooted in presence.

Today invites you to honor your embodied truth ~ the knowing that exists beyond logic, the expression that rises from your bones, breath, belly.

The archetype of the day is The Inner Bodykeeper ~ the part of you that holds the memory, the emotion, the knowing… and waits for your permission to finally release it with love.

Today's Symbols::

- A ribcage drawn open to reveal a blooming heart, full and unguarded
- Hematite, for grounding, truth embodiment, and root chakra strength
- The Judgement card, awakening to self, rising not in sound but in soul
- A horse standing still in rain, unmoving, fully present, deeply felt

Reflection Prompts:

- What truth has my body been holding ~ that my words haven't yet spoken?

- Where do I feel emotion physically? What lives in my chest, my gut, my shoulders?
- What happens when I stop explaining and just let my body speak?

Integration Practice: The Body Speaks Ritual

With a partner:

- Sit back to back.
- One person speaks from the body:

"My chest says…" "My breath wants…" "My skin remembers…"

- Then switch.
- No fixing, just witnessing.

Alone:

- Stand or lie down.
- Ask out loud:

"Body, what are you trying to tell me?"

- Move intuitively ~ stretch, shake, weep, rest.
- Then whisper: *"I hear you now. I believe you."*

Closing Mantra for the Today ~

"My truth lives in more than words. I feel it. I carry it. I let it move. My body is my story ~ sacred, whole, and worthy of being heard."

May 27 – The Day of Mutual Awakening

A story of shared transformation, mirrored growth, and the sacred power of intimacy that not only connects ~ but evolves both souls at once

There once was a soul who believed awakening had to be a solo journey.

They read the books. Sat in silence. Felt things shift inside them ~ but also felt alone in it.

They loved deeply, yes ~ but from a distance.

Their partner was kind. Present. Devoted.

But still, the soul kept the deepest parts of their evolution private ~ as if growth meant *leaving*, or as if becoming more meant risking *being too much*.

Then one day ~ as the Northern sunrise warmed fields into new gold, or the Southern night wrapped trees in sacred stillness ~ they shared something that felt raw:

"I've changed. I'm changing."

They said it with fear. But their partner didn't pull away. They leaned closer.

And to their surprise, their partner said:

"So am I. Let's grow in the same direction ~ even if the paths are wild."

In that moment, something opened between them ~ a third space.

Not them. Not the other. But *us* ~ the place where two awakenings became *one unfolding*.

May 27 carries the energy of 9 (2 + 7), the number of culmination, spiritual maturity, and transformative connection.

Today invites you into mutual awakening ~ the sacred invitation to grow with someone, not away from them, and to see intimacy as a container for shared evolution.

The archetype of the day is The Mirrored Flame ~ the self who reflects and receives transformation not alone, but *alongside*, letting intimacy become the soil for soul-deep change.

Today's Symbols::

- Two spirals intertwining, neither overtaking the other
- Lapis lazuli, for shared insight, deep conversation, and spiritual partnership
- The Two of Wands, choosing growth with open eyes and shared fire
- A pair of eagles flying in sync, separate yet aligned, eyes on the horizon

Reflection Prompts:
- What part of me is awakening ~ and have I shared that with someone I love?
- Do I fear growing in front of others ~ or letting others grow without me?
- How can I invite someone into my evolution, not to follow, but to walk beside?

Integration Practice: The Shared Becoming

With a partner:
- Sit or lie facing one another.
- Take turns answering:

"Here's how I've changed lately…" "Here's what I hope we can grow into together…"

Then hold silence for one minute ~ hands connected, eyes soft.

Alone:
- Write two journal entries:
  - *"Who I was six months ago…"
  - *"Who I'm becoming ~ and who I want beside me as I do."*

Let your growth be witnessed ~ by you, or by someone worthy.

Closing Mantra for the Today ~

"I evolve without leaving. I awaken beside those who meet me in the mystery. Love is not where change ends ~ it is where it expands."

May 28 – The Day of Sensual Grace

A story of fluid movement, embodied elegance, and the sacred sensuality that emerges not through effort ~ but through being fully at home in your body

There once was a soul who thought sensuality had to be loud.

They believed it came with red lips, dramatic moves, breathless tension. They tried to perform it. Channel it. *Master* it.

But something always felt a little… disconnected.

It wasn't that they weren't sensual. It's that they didn't yet know how to be *graceful with their own desire*.

Then one day ~ as the Northern air shimmered through flowering branches, or the Southern world stilled before a coming rain ~ the soul walked across the room with no one watching.

Barefoot. Unrushed. Present.

And in the way their hips moved ~ in the way their chest rose and fell ~ they felt it:

"This… this is my grace. This is sensuality ~ not as performance, but as presence."

They didn't need approval. They didn't need choreography.

They simply needed to *let themselves feel beautiful from within.*

May 28 carries the energy of 1 (2 + 8 = 10 → 1), the number of self-initiation, confidence, and rooted presence.

Today is about claiming your sensual grace ~ not the version you've been taught to show others, but the version that lives quietly in your breath, your stride, your *being.*

The archetype of the day is The Sensual Sovereign ~ the self who walks with awareness, touches with elegance, and knows that softness can be strength, and slowness can be magnetic.

Today's Symbols::

- A scarf floating through air as someone twirls slowly, unhurried and soft
- Rose quartz + moonstone, for loving presence and graceful embodiment
- The Empress, fertile, grounded, radiant without demand
- A cat stretching across sun-warmed stone, sensual, quiet, unbothered

Reflection Prompts:

- What does sensual grace look and feel like to me ~ when no one's watching?

- Where have I tried to perform beauty instead of inhabit it?
- How can I embody elegance, not as perfection ~ but as grounded self-expression?

Integration Practice: The Grace Walk

With a partner:

- Invite each other to move slowly through the space ~ a hallway, a bedroom, a garden ~ in full awareness of the body.
- No goal. No seduction. Just *presence*.
- Watch each other with admiration, not analysis.

Alone:

- Put on music that makes your body want to *melt*.
- Dance. Walk. Stretch.
- Say aloud:

"This is my grace. I don't need to be watched to feel radiant."

Let sensuality become an inward state ~ not a show.

Closing Mantra for the Today ~

"I move in beauty. I touch with care. I carry grace in my breath, my hips, my presence ~ because I belong to myself."

May 29 – The Day of Sacred Memory

A story of emotional echoes, intimate recall, and the deep sensuality of remembering not just with the mind ~ but with the body and the soul

There once was a soul who kept their memories tucked away.

Tied in neat boxes. Labeled with logic. Visited only when necessary ~ never too often, never too deep.

They thought healing meant forgetting. They thought moving on required erasing the texture of what had once been real.

But then one evening ~ as the Northern sky glowed with gold-tinged clouds, or the Southern twilight turned cool and violet across bare trees ~ a scent drifted through the open window.

It stopped them. Not with pain ~ but with *presence*.

The smell of skin after rain. The faint trace of something once whispered. A memory that lived not in thought ~ but in *touch*, in *tone*, in the *soft ache* of something meaningful.

They didn't flinch. They didn't drown.

They *honored* it.

"This," the soul thought, "is a sacred memory ~ not to hold onto, but to hold *with grace*."

May 29 carries the energy of 2 (2 + 9 = 11 → 1 + 1 = 2), the number of reflection, emotional duality, and tender presence.

Today asks you to explore your sacred memories ~ not just as recollections, but as portals to intimacy, identity, and evolution.

The archetype of the day is The Keeper of Feeling ~ the self who remembers not to cling, but to feel deeply, then release with reverence.

Today's Symbols::

- A photograph with a hand resting gently atop it, eyes closed
- Labradorite, for intuitive memory, emotional clarity, and shadow-light balance
- The Six of Cups, nostalgia, past emotion, and memory as a healing bridge
- A swan drifting past a familiar shore, pausing ~ but not landing

Reflection Prompts:

- What memory has been surfacing lately ~ and why might it be returning now?
- What touch, scent, or moment from my past still lives in my body?

- Can I let myself remember without needing to return ~ and feel without needing to fix?

Integration Practice: Memory Ritual

With a partner:

- Share a moment from your shared history ~ something small, sensory, sacred.

"I remember the sound of your voice that night..." "I still feel the way your hand brushed mine at the door..."

Let the memory live between you like a candle ~ not reignited, just warmed.

Alone:

- Light a candle.
- Recall a memory that shaped your capacity to love or feel deeply.
- Say aloud:

"Thank you for the way you made me feel. I carry it with grace, not weight."
Then exhale. Let it drift.

Closing Mantra for the Today ~

"My memories are sacred visitors. I let them pass through me with reverence. I do not erase the past ~ I soften around it."

May 30 – The Day of Erotic Stillness

A story of magnetic quiet, breath-held desire, and the sacred power of connection that deepens not in movement ~ but in presence

There once was a soul who thought desire lived only in action.

In movement. In rhythm. In the tangible. They associated stillness with absence. Quiet with distance.

But one evening ~ as the Northern sun slowed over lavender fields, or the Southern sky wrapped the world in cool indigo hush ~ they sat with their partner, side by side, bodies just barely touching.

There was no kiss. No urgency. Only the soft electricity of *being still… together*. And something stirred.

A breath. A pause. The heat in the silence between.

"This," the soul whispered inwardly, "is stillness that doesn't empty ~ it *awakens*."

And in that stillness, the hunger didn't vanish ~ it *deepened*. Not as a need to act, but as a willingness to stay.

To *feel* before reaching. To *receive* without taking. To *desire* without demand.

May 30 carries the energy of 3 (3 + 0), the number of embodied expression, magnetic stillness, and sensual communication without words.

Today is an invitation into erotic stillness ~ a form of intimacy that exists in the pause before the touch, in the gaze before the move, in the breath that lingers between two connected hearts.

The archetype of the day is The Silent Flame ~ the self who knows that heat does not always require motion, and that some of the deepest intimacy arises from what is *not done*, but simply *felt*.

Today's Symbols::

- Two figures seated in stillness, foreheads nearly touching, eyes closed
- Obsidian, for grounding erotic energy and containing intensity with clarity
- The Four of Swords, a sacred pause, healing rest, and intentional space
- A panther lying perfectly still, eyes alert, every nerve alive

Reflection Prompts:

- What happens in me when things grow still ~ especially in moments of intimacy?

- Do I rush closeness out of fear the silence means something is missing?
- What might stillness reveal about my capacity to feel without doing?

Integration Practice: The Stillness Ritual

With a partner:

- Sit facing one another. Knees touching. Eyes closed or gently open.
- No words. No touch beyond what arises naturally.
- Breathe in sync for 3–5 minutes. Let the stillness speak.
- Afterward, share just one word to describe what you felt.

Alone:

- Lie down in soft light or darkness.
- Place one hand on your belly, one on your heart.
- Breathe.
- Whisper:

"I am enough in this moment. I do not need to move to feel."

This is erotic presence ~ sacred, steady, still.

Closing Mantra for the Today ~

"I am not empty in stillness. I am alive, aware, and open. Desire breathes here ~ without pressure, without urgency."

May 31 – The Day of Intimate Renewal

A story of soft endings, soul reawakening, and the sacred moment where love isn't restarted ~ but remembered, revived, and met with new breath

There once was a soul who thought intimacy had to be constant to be real.

That desire should never fade. That closeness should always feel electric. That if passion dulled ~ something must be broken.

So when stillness came, or silence stretched longer than usual… they worried.

But one dusk ~ as the Northern air thickened with jasmine and open windows, or the Southern sky folded into early dark with gentle winds ~ the soul and their partner lit a candle, not for ritual… just for *reminder*.

They didn't talk about the distance. They didn't analyze the past. They simply sat. Touched fingertips. And shared a quiet, honest smile.

No performance. No pressure. Just presence.

And something returned ~ not suddenly, but *softly*.

The thread of love that had always been there beneath the layers of life, now rising like breath on a still morning.

"This," the soul whispered, "is how love renews ~ not by force, but by *remembering*."

May 31 carries the energy of 4 (3 + 1), the number of stability, gentle grounding, and rebuilding intimacy with care.

Today invites you into intimate renewal ~ not by starting over, but by returning *with softness* to what already lives beneath the surface.

The archetype of the day is The Rekindler ~ the part of you that knows love isn't a flame that burns constantly, but one that *glows quietly until reignited with presence*.

Today's Symbols::

- A single flame between two joined hands, calm, steady, renewed
- Garnet, for revitalizing love, rooting desire, and sustaining passion over time
- The Six of Pentacles, mutual giving, balance restored, slow regrowth
- A phoenix rising not in fire ~ but in light, glowing softly in golden mist

Reflection Prompts:

- Where in my intimate life am I being called to renew ~ not recreate?
- What needs tenderness, breath, or attention... not change, but care?
- What happens when I meet love where it is, not where it used to be?

Integration Practice: Gentle Return

With a partner:

- Ask one another:

"What do you miss ~ not from the past, but from us?"

- Share gently. Then choose one small action to rekindle your closeness today.

A meal. A bath. A long-held hug.

- No fixing. Just *returning*.

Alone:

- Light a candle and speak aloud to your own heart:

"What part of me longs to be remembered?"

- Write down one memory of self-love, confidence, or connection ~ and then recreate one element of it today.

Closing Mantra for the Today ~

"I do not need to start over. I only need to return. Love is here ~ still breathing, still becoming."

May Reflection

Opening Through Intimacy

This month, you've been invited into the living world of intimacy ~ not just sexual, but emotional, sensory, and soulful.

You've explored closeness in all its forms: the moment a breath syncs, the quiet that holds a truth, the touch that says *"I see you."*

But more than anything, May asked you to stay inside your own body and heart ~ even while reaching for another.

Now, as the month closes, we ask: What has opened? What has softened? What is asking to stay?

Journal Prompts for May Integration

You may wish to write your reflections across several days ~ or speak them aloud to yourself or your partner. Use the prompts that follow as a monthly intimacy check-in.

💬 1. Emotional Honesty

— Did I speak one truth this month that I usually keep hidden?

— When was I emotionally available, and when did I pull away? Why?

Practical Practice: Revisit one conversation you had this month. What could be said now, with more honesty or clarity? Write the sentence or speak it aloud, even if just to yourself.

🫂 2. Sensory Presence

— What moment of pure presence stands out most this month?

— Which of my five senses felt most alive in intimacy ~ and which felt ignored?

Practical Practice: Choose one evening this week to eat, touch, and breathe with full awareness. No multitasking. No background noise. Let it be sacred through attention.

🛏 3. Physical Connection

— How did I approach physical closeness? With reverence? Routine? Resistance?

- Did I give and receive touch in a way that felt mutual and meaningful?

Practical Practice: Create a touch ritual with your partner or yourself. No goal. Just 10 minutes of skin-to-skin presence ~ palms on back, forehead to forehead, or tracing fingertips with intention.

4. Self-Love and Body Trust

- What part of my body asked for love this month ~ and did I listen?
- Did I meet my own desire with kindness, curiosity, or shame?

Practical Practice: Stand before a mirror. Place a hand on your heart, another on your belly. Whisper: *"You are allowed to feel. You are allowed to want. I trust you."*

5. Relational Renewal

- Was there a moment I felt disconnected in love ~ and what helped me return?
- What small action revived connection or tenderness?

Practical Practice: Schedule a "touch base" evening. Light a candle. Share one thing you appreciated and one thing you longed for in the past 30 days ~ no blame, only truth.

◎ Thematic Review: Tracing the Numbers

Notice how the repeating numbers in May deepened your rhythm:

- The 2s asked you to reflect and receive: May 2, 11, 20, 29
- The 5s brought emotional and erotic liberation: May 5, 14, 23
- The 7s returned you to inner listening: May 7, 16, 25

What patterns did you notice? What stories did you start to unwrite… or rewrite?

✺ Sacred Questions to Close May

You may write, meditate on, or speak these aloud in stillness.

- How has my definition of intimacy changed this month?
- Do I feel more at home in my body ~ or more aware of the places I still hold back?
- Where can I invite more reverence into my relationships ~ not grand gestures, but small sacred moments?
- What do I want to carry forward into June ~ not as a challenge, but as a rhythm?

🔄 Suggested End-of-Month Ritual:

"The Return to Touch"

- Light a candle ~ preferably one used earlier in the month.
- Sit or lie somewhere quiet. Bring a journal, or your partner.
- Place your hand over your chest and speak aloud:

"I return not to the beginning ~ but to the part of me that never stopped longing. I do not rush. I do not perform. I return, gently… to presence."

- Write (or share) the phrase:

"This month, I learned that love can look like…" and let the sentence complete itself.

Let this be your doorway into June.

June 1 – The Day of Body Wisdom

A story of physical intuition, cellular knowing, and remembering that the body doesn't speak in logic ~ it speaks in movement, tension, and sacred yes/no

There once was a soul who trusted their thoughts above all else.

They made lists. Weighed pros and cons. Asked others for advice. Calculated. Measured. Reconsidered.

But when it came to decisions that mattered ~ the ones that felt like doorways, relationships, touch ~ nothing ever quite clicked.

Until one morning ~ as the Northern Hemisphere burst with light, green, and restless warmth, or the Southern world withdrew into breath-fogged windows and inward days ~ the soul woke early.

They stretched. Breathed. Felt a tension in their neck, a heaviness in their gut.

And instead of overriding it, they *listened*.

They stepped outside ~ into sun, or wind, or chill ~ and let the earth reflect what their mind could not.

"This," the soul thought, "is what my body has been trying to tell me ~ even when I wouldn't listen."

And in that moment, a quiet clarity arrived ~ not as words, but as felt truth.

Seasonal Awareness::

🌕 In the Northern Hemisphere, nature is *rising* ~ calling your body into expression, energy, and outward flow. Let this be the season where your body initiates choices, not just follows.

🌑 In the Southern Hemisphere, the world is *contracting* ~ inviting stillness, warmth, internal rest, and careful movement. Let your body be a sanctuary, not a tool for productivity.

Wherever you are, your body holds a seasonal mirror: listen for the rhythm *within the climate you're living in.*

Echoes from Earlier Days::

- On January 1, you learned the sacred power of beginning in stillness.
- On March 4, you were reminded to trust the wisdom of grounding.
- On May 7, you surrendered into trust ~ not just in others, but in your nervous system.

Today continues that rhythm ~ inviting you to move from the inside out.

Archetype of the Day: *The Embodied Knower*

This is the part of you that does not wait for approval. That does not seek evidence. That *feels something in the bones and trusts it enough to act.*

You've carried this wisdom since before you had words ~ now is the time to listen again.

Today's Symbols:

- A bare foot pressed into warm soil or cool wood, steady and awake
- Tiger's eye, for inner alignment, decision-making, and grounded action
- The High Priestess, not of mystery today ~ but of *embodied knowing*
- A tree standing alone on a ridge, roots deep, leaves still

Reflection Prompts:

- Where in my life have I been ignoring what my body already knows?
- What happens when I stop asking for signs and start asking for sensations?
- If I moved today based on inner alignment ~ not external pressure ~ what would shift?

Integration Practice: Yes / No Body Scan

Find a quiet space. Sit or lie down. Close your eyes.

Ask your body a few yes/no questions ~ not with words, but with awareness:

- "Is this path right for me ~ today?"
- "Is this relationship expanding or constricting me?"

Let your body answer. Does your chest open or close? Does your breath deepen or tighten? Does your spine straighten or slump?

This is not analysis. This is *reverence*.

If you're in the Northern Hemisphere, take a walk afterward ~ let your body lead. If you're in the Southern Hemisphere, wrap yourself in something warm and journal:

"My body wants me to know…"

Closing Mantra for the Today ~

"My body is not separate from my soul. It speaks with sensation, rhythm, and knowing. I listen, I move, I trust what lives beneath my thinking."

June 2 – The Day of Erotic Simplicity

A story of quiet touch, honest want, and the deep pleasure that arises not from intensity ~ but from ease, trust, and soulful uncluttering

There once was a soul who believed eroticism had to be elaborate.

Candles. Lingerie. Choreography. They'd read the books. Followed the scripts. They tried to do it all "right."

But something always felt one step removed ~ as if they were *performing* pleasure rather than *living it*.

Then one morning ~ as the Northern fields warmed with early sunlight or the Southern winds gathered softly under a thick blanket sky ~ the soul stirred awake.

Their partner's hand was already resting gently on their hip.

No words. No expectation. Just presence. Just warmth. Just that soft, undeniable message:

"I'm here ~ and so are you."

They didn't rush. They didn't even move much.

Instead, they breathed. And in the stillness, something bloomed:

"This is enough. This is not minimal ~ it's meaningful."

And the soul realized: Simplicity doesn't mean lack. It means *clarity. Ease. Unforced connection.*

Seasonal Awareness:

🌗 In the Northern Hemisphere, warmth expands your senses. Let your skin breathe. Let your body slow. Let eroticism come not from *effort*, but from *ease* ~ fresh air, bare feet, light meals, and laughter under open skies.

🌑 In the Southern Hemisphere, colder days may restrict movement, but they invite deeper stillness. Let desire come through texture, closeness, and low-effort, high-trust intimacy. Erotic simplicity might be the heat of shared breath, the pulse of touch under blankets.

Simplicity is the shared language of both climates ~ the permission to *not perform*, and still feel everything.

Echoes from Earlier Days:

- On May 4, you discovered erotic presence as slowness, not speed.
- On May 10, you explored sacred touch through still hands.
- On March 18, you learned that less noise often brings more clarity.

Today continues that rhythm ~ stripping intimacy back to what *actually matters.*

Archetype of the Day: *The Bare-Skin Beloved*

This part of you knows that pleasure doesn't require preparation. It only asks for *permission* ~ to be soft, to be unpolished, to be here.

Today's Symbols:

— A white linen sheet crumpled at the edge of a bed, still warm

— Pink Himalayan salt, simple, grounding, pure

— The Two of Cups, not dramatic love ~ but *real*, balanced, sacred sharing

— A fox curled in a patch of sun, alert but unhurried

Reflection Prompts:

— Where have I overcomplicated intimacy ~ and what might it look like if I simplified it today?

— What kind of closeness do I crave when I drop the performance?

— Can I let myself be wanted as I am ~ no scripts, no edits, no effort?

Integration Practice: The 3-Point Simplicity Ritual

With a partner:

— Sit or lie in a quiet space.

- Choose just three points of touch ~ hand to chest, lips to forehead, fingers on arm.
- Breathe. Hold. Listen. No need to move beyond that.

Say aloud:

"We don't need to do more. We just need to be here."

Alone:

- Light a candle. Wrap yourself in your softest garment.
- Touch your own skin with gratitude ~ no stimulation, just *contact*.
- Whisper:

"This is enough. I am enough. Simplicity is sacred."

Closing Mantra for the Today ~

"I release performance. I return to presence. In stillness, in breath, in the ordinary ~ I find the erotic again."

June 3 – The Day of Loving Clarity

A story of honest seeing, soul-aligned boundaries, and the kind of intimacy that thrives not in fog ~ but in fearless understanding

There once was a soul who loved deeply... but often at the cost of their clarity.

They excused things. Overlooked the ache in their chest. Confused comfort with closeness. They thought love meant softening their own knowing to make space for another.

But one day ~ as the Northern world swelled with summer's confident bloom, or the Southern trees stood bare in exquisite detail ~ the soul received a message they didn't expect:

It wasn't harsh. It wasn't loud. It simply said:

"Love that obscures your truth isn't love ~ it's a fog."

They paused. Looked around. And suddenly, what had been confusing became crystal clear.

They could see what they had been avoiding. They could feel the places where truth had been sacrificed for harmony.

And instead of shaming themselves, they blessed the seeing.

"This," the soul whispered, "is loving clarity ~ not to push others away, but to finally come home to myself."

Seasonal Awareness:

🌕 In the Northern Hemisphere, nature is revealing itself boldly ~ petals open, skies clear, shadows short.

Let this mirror your relationships. Let *truth bloom*. Name what's real.

🌑 In the Southern Hemisphere, the bareness of winter strips everything down to the essentials. This is not about confrontation ~ but *about courageous honesty*. Love that endures winter is love that sees clearly.

Wherever you are, clarity is *not a threat to connection*. It is what makes deeper connection *possible*.

Echoes from Earlier Days:

- On February 19, you were invited to walk with truth rather than run from it.
- On May 19, you honored sacred boundaries in love.
- On March 7, you began to ask what your relationships were reflecting back to you.

June 3 continues this rhythm ~ but sharpens it. You now have the emotional maturity to see clearly and still stay *soft*.

Archetype of the Day: *The Clear-Hearted Lover*

This is the self who brings honesty into closeness ~ not to divide, but to refine. Who knows that saying the true thing might feel risky… but never cruel.

Symbols of the Day::

- A window washed clean with sunlight pouring through, no curtains, no filter
- Clear quartz, for spiritual vision, emotional purification, and truth amplification
- The Justice card, balanced clarity, fairness in love, and right alignment
- A falcon gliding with focused eyes, cutting through clouds

Reflection Prompts:

- Where in love am I seeing clearly for the first time ~ and what truth is emerging?
- Is there a part of me that still fears clarity will lead to loss?
- How might I express truth with tenderness ~ not silence or sharpness, but softness with strength?

Integration Practice: Clarity with Compassion

With a partner:

- Each write one sentence that begins:

"Something I've been hesitant to say, but is true for me…"

- Share gently, without defense.
- The other responds:

"Thank you for your clarity. I'm listening."

Alone:

- Journal:

"What I've always known, but only now trust myself to say is…"

- Write it. Then speak it aloud in front of a mirror ~ to yourself, with love.

Closing Mantra for the Today ~

"My clarity is a gift ~ to myself and to those I love. I do not abandon truth for comfort. I speak what is real ~ with reverence."

June 4 – The Day of Rooted Sensuality

A story of embodied grounding, slow pleasure, and remembering that the deepest desire doesn't float ~ it lives in the soil of your being

There once was a soul who chased ecstasy like a wind.

They reached for highs. They wanted intensity. They moved fast ~ always looking for more.

And yet, after the passion passed… they often felt *untethered*.

Until one afternoon ~ as the Northern fields warmed under heavy summer sun, or the Southern earth curled into deep rest beneath frostbitten grass ~ they stood barefoot in the dirt.

Their body quieted. Their breath slowed. And in that moment, a realization rose up from the ground beneath them:

"I don't need to rise to find pleasure. I need to *root into it*."

The pulse of the earth matched the rhythm of their hips. The wind wrapped their limbs like a lover. The warmth of stillness became an invitation ~ not to chase, but to *sink*.

And the soul remembered: Sensuality isn't about escape. It's about presence. Contact. Trusting the *ground* you're standing on.

Seasonal Awareness:

🌑 In the Northern Hemisphere, summer is awakening the body. Let your sensuality express through slow movement, bare skin, grounded walks, and touch that starts from the feet up. Root, then rise.

🌑 In the Southern Hemisphere, winter draws your attention inward. Sensuality here is deep warmth, weighty blankets, warm oils, and sacred stillness. Let desire be a slow ember, not a firestorm.

Pleasure isn't always light and air. Sometimes, it's the *soil itself.*

Echoes from Earlier Days:

— On February 4, you first practiced presence through the soles of your feet.

— On April 8, you invited your body to speak through slowness.

— On May 17, you learned sacred slowness as a love language.

Today returns to that truth ~ but now with embodiment, not just reflection.

Archetype of the Day: *The Sensual Root*

This part of you trusts that pleasure does not need to rise quickly ~ it grows with time, with trust, and with contact to what's real.

You don't have to float. You can bloom *in place*.

Symbols of the Day:

- Bare feet pressing into moss, toes curling with subtle delight
- Red jasper, for root chakra grounding, vitality, and body-confidence
- The Knight of Pentacles, steady, sensual, devoted to the present moment
- A wild sow resting in a patch of sun, full-bodied and unashamed

Reflection Prompts:

- Where do I still chase pleasure as a way of leaving myself ~ rather than entering more deeply into my body?
- What would it feel like to slow down and let desire rise from the ground up?
- Which parts of me are longing for contact ~ not intensity, but deep, rooted sensuality?

Integration Practice: The Root Ritual

With a partner:

- Sit cross-legged, knees touching.

- Place hands on each other's thighs or hips ~ low, steady, grounded.
- Breathe in sync. Don't move quickly. Let stillness speak.

Say aloud:

"We meet here. In our weight. In our realness. In our roots."

Alone:

- Stand barefoot if possible.
- Place both hands over your belly and hips.
- Gently press your feet into the floor and whisper:

"I return to my root. I do not rise to escape ~ I rise from here."

Closing Mantra for the Today ~

"My pleasure is rooted, not rushed. I feel safe in my skin. My desire begins where I touch the earth."

June 5 – The Day of Wild Permission

A story of untamed truth, embodied risk, and the power that awakens when you give yourself full permission to feel, want, and choose without apology

There once was a soul who had tamed themselves to be loved.

They dimmed their fire. They quieted their wants. They smiled when they longed to scream, stayed still when their body wanted to move.

They were praised for being easy, agreeable, composed.

But one day ~ as the Northern grasses swayed in golden riot, or the Southern trees stood stripped and unapologetic in winter's stark beauty ~ the soul saw a fox dart across the path.

It didn't ask for permission. It didn't explain its speed. It moved because it *needed* to ~ and because it could.

The soul felt something primal stir.

And for the first time in a long time, they asked:

"What part of me have I caged to be accepted? And what would happen if I let it run free ~ just once?"

Seasonal Awareness:

🌑 In the Northern Hemisphere, wildness comes easy now ~ heat rises, days lengthen, energy surges. Let your body move fast, sweat, laugh loudly, take space.

🌑 In the Southern Hemisphere, winter invites quieter rebellion. Let your wildness show up in bold truth, emotional heat, permission to rest when the world demands more.

Wherever you are, wildness isn't recklessness ~ it's the choice to be whole.

Echoes from Earlier Days:

— On January 11, you challenged your inner restraint.
— On March 15, you allowed honest anger to rise.
— On May 23, you explored erotic self-trust.

Today deepens that invitation ~ from whispering permission… to *embodying it*.

Archetype of the Day: *The Untamed Heart*

This is the self who no longer asks for space ~ they *take* it, reverently. They know that wildness is not disruption ~ it's *remembrance*.

They run toward what feels right, even if no one claps.

Symbols of the Day:

- A wild animal's tracks across loose soil, fresh and uncontained
- Carnelian, for boldness, creativity, permission to desire and act
- The Strength card, not in taming the beast ~ but becoming one with it
- A wind-tossed mane, full of motion, power, and freedom

Reflection Prompts:

- Where have I tamed myself to fit ~ in love, in pleasure, in truth?
- What do I long to do, say, or feel that still scares me ~ but also excites me?
- What part of me needs wild permission today ~ not forever, just for now?

Integration Practice: A Small Act of Sacred Wildness
With a partner:

- Share one unfiltered desire, impulse, or idea that you've been afraid to speak.

- Let your body express it ~ through dance, words, breath, or closeness.
- Say together:

"I honor the wild in you. I do not ask it to shrink."

Alone:

- Write the sentence:

"If I weren't afraid of being too much, I would…"

- Complete it. Then go do a version of it ~ even if it's small.
- Shout. Cry. Move. Rest. Break a pattern.

This is your permission slip.

Closing Mantra for the Today ~

"I do not apologize for being whole. I do not cage the sacred animal within. My wildness is wisdom ~ and today, I let it breathe."

June 6 – The Day of Devotional Desire

A story of sacred longing, soulful surrender, and remembering that true desire isn't chaos ~ it's consecrated, clarifying, and holy when held with heart

There once was a soul who had learned to distrust their desire.

They had been told it was selfish. Messy. Too much.

So they buried it. Repackaged it as politeness. Starved it into control.

But deep within them, something ancient still stirred ~ a longing that wasn't reckless… just *real*.

Then one dusk ~ as the Northern sun dipped into the haze of high summer, or the Southern fire crackled beside wool-wrapped shoulders ~ the soul knelt, not in shame, but in reverence.

They whispered, not to a god, but to the fire within them:

"I want what is mine to feel. I want it fully. I want it faithfully."

And in that quiet invocation, their desire shifted shape ~ from hunger into offering. From shame into *devotion*.

It was no longer something to control ~ but something to *honor*.

Seasonal Awareness:

◐ In the Northern Hemisphere, summer heat may heighten desire. Let it move through your senses ~ not just sexually, but through joy, creativity, beauty, and touch. Devote yourself to *what delights you*.

◐ In the Southern Hemisphere, the inward season makes room for subtle, slow-burning longing. Let your devotion be gentle, embodied through ritual, stillness, whispered prayer. *Desire doesn't need volume ~ only truth*.

Echoes from Earlier Days:

- On February 14, you learned love as a form of listening.
- On May 13, you practiced sensual receiving without guilt.
- On May 31, you remembered that intimacy is renewed, not restarted.

Today asks you not to chase desire ~ but to bow to it. To let it be holy.

Archetype of the Day: *The Sacred Desirer*

This is the self who knows that longing, when aligned, is *devotion in motion*. They ask, they reach, they ache ~ not out of lack, but from reverence for what *wants to move through them*.

Symbols of the Day:

- A candlelit bowl of water with rose petals, still and intentional
- Ruby, for heart-centered desire, passion, and soul-anchored love
- The Knight of Cups, romantic yet grounded, brave in pursuit of emotional truth
- A black horse bowing its head, powerful yet humble

Reflection Prompts:

- What do I truly desire ~ beyond performance or reaction?
- Where have I confused craving with chaos, and how can I honor longing as guidance?
- How would it feel to offer my desire like a prayer ~ sacred, sensual, and sovereign?

Integration Practice: Devotional Desire Ritual
With a partner:

- Sit face-to-face in stillness.
- Speak your desires aloud, not as demands ~ but as invitations.

- Begin each phrase with:

"What I long for with you is…"

- Breathe. Touch. Listen without fixing.

Alone:

- Write your desires as offerings, not goals.

"Today, I offer myself the desire to…"

- Light a candle.
- Place your hand on your heart. Whisper:

"This desire is sacred. I am worthy of wanting."

Closing Mantra for the Today ~

"My desire is not shameful ~ it is sacred. I honor what I long for with devotion, not apology. This is holy fire ~ and I trust it to lead me."

June 7 – The Day of Soulful Submission

A story of sacred surrender, mutual safety, and the profound power that arises when yielding is not weakness ~ but a conscious act of love and trust

There once was a soul who had always stayed in control.

They led. Held it together. Protected their heart with precision and poise. They thought surrender meant giving up. Meant vulnerability they couldn't afford.

But one night ~ as the Northern air pulsed with summer's thick invitation, or the Southern fire dimmed to glowing embers in a quiet room ~ the soul felt something shift.

They were held ~ not just physically, but emotionally. Their partner's hands were firm, but their presence was reverent. And for the first time, the soul didn't resist. They *relented*.

Not out of powerlessness... but out of *powerful trust*.

"This," they thought, "is not submission to another ~ this is submission to *truth*."

And in that yielding, they felt more free, more loved, and more whole than they ever did in control.

Seasonal Awareness:

🌑 In the Northern Hemisphere, summer's energy can invite bold expression ~ but within that, there's also the invitation to soften, to let go, to trust pleasure without pushing.

🌑 In the Southern Hemisphere, winter encourages the inward pull ~ and with it, the sacred art of being held, of receiving not just touch, but care, space, and surrender.

Wherever you are, submission today is not about giving up power ~ it's about consciously offering it where you feel safe, seen, and sacred.

Echoes from Earlier Days:

- On January 18, you reflected on emotional surrender.
- On May 12, you felt the power of intimate trust.
- On June 1, you learned to listen to the truth of your body's yes and no.

Today brings those teachings into embodiment ~ through *conscious yielding*.

Archetype of the Day: *The Sacred Receiver*

This is the self who knows surrender is not passivity ~ it's presence. They lean into love without losing themselves. They allow, not because they must, but because it is *safe to soften*.

Symbols of the Day:

- A silk ribbon gently untied, soft, slow, consensual
- Moonstone, for divine feminine energy, emotional release, and intuition
- The Hanged Man, offering perspective through surrender, not defeat
- A lioness laying her head in another's lap, trusting, whole, at peace

Reflection Prompts:

- Where in my life do I resist surrender ~ and what is that resistance protecting?
- What would it look like to submit by choice, in love, in intimacy, in healing?
- Can I trust myself enough to let go ~ and still remain whole?

Integration Practice: Surrender with Sovereignty
With a partner:

- Before physical closeness, agree on the theme: "I am held. I am choosing to let go."
- Let one person lead, the other yield ~ fully present, fully consensual.

- Afterward, debrief:

"What part of you felt seen?" "What part of me felt free?"

Alone:

- Light a candle. Lie down with arms open, palms up.
- Breathe deeply.
- Say aloud:

"I surrender to what is loving. I release what is forced. I am safe to rest. I am safe to receive."

Closing Mantra for the Today ~

"I do not lose myself in surrender. I become more of who I am ~ in softness, in stillness, in sacred trust."

June 8 – The Day of Grounded Passion

A story of stable heat, embodied presence, and remembering that desire doesn't always roar ~ sometimes, it roots itself deeply and burns slow and steady

There once was a soul who confused passion with chaos.

They sought fire that consumed. They craved love that was wild, erratic, and all-consuming. They mistook volatility for vitality.

And for a time, it felt alive ~ until it didn't. Until they were left burned out, unanchored, hollowed by what never lasted.

Then one morning ~ as the Northern sun cast golden heat over calm fields, or the Southern air stilled with the weight of deep winter silence ~ they lay beside someone who didn't rush them, excite them wildly, or challenge their nervous system.

Instead, this person stayed.

And in the steadiness of that gaze, the warmth of that hand, the ease of being known ~ the soul felt something even more powerful than intensity:

"This is passion that knows where it lives. This is fire that *nourishes*, not scorches."

And for the first time, the soul let themselves be warmed ~ not whipped into frenzy.

Seasonal Awareness:

◎ In the Northern Hemisphere, your body may be craving movement, stimulation, adventure ~ let that energy be rooted in rituals that ground your nervous system while still expanding pleasure.

◎ In the Southern Hemisphere, colder days are asking you to slow down. Passion becomes less about spark and more about *embers* ~ held close, tended with care, burning beneath the surface.

Today's lesson lives in the middle: passion that is sustainable, sensual, and safe.

Echoes from Earlier Days:

— On April 2, you met your inner flame and learned to tend it with care.

— On May 14, you explored soul-made sex ~ where depth meets desire.

— On June 4, you rooted your sensuality into the ground.

Today, all those lessons converge: heat with roots. Desire with devotion.

Archetype of the Day: *The Steady Flame*

This self doesn't need drama to feel desire. They don't chase ~ they *cultivate*. They understand that the deepest passion is not fragile... it's forged.

Symbols of the Day:

— A clay hearth with a fire burning low, tended with love
— Garnet, for grounded vitality, deep attraction, and emotional endurance
— The King of Wands, radiant, rooted, magnetic through inner authority
— A mountain fox resting on warm stone, alert, powerful, unshaken

Reflection Prompts:

— Have I been confusing instability with chemistry ~ and what does true passion feel like in my body?
— Where in my life could I create more space for grounded desire to flourish?
— What might shift if I stop chasing the spark and start building the flame?

Integration Practice: The Slow-Burn Ritual

With a partner:

- Spend 15 minutes touching each other without arousal as a goal.
- Focus on warmth, skin, breath ~ no performance, just presence.
- Say aloud:

"We tend the flame. We don't need to rush the fire."

Alone:

- Wrap yourself in warmth.
- Light a candle. Place one hand on your belly, one on your chest.
- Breathe. Visualize your passion as a fire that begins inside you ~ deep, enduring.
- Whisper:

"I am allowed to burn slow and steady. My passion is sacred and sustainable."

Closing Mantra for the Today ~

"I do not chase the spark ~ I tend the flame. I do not burn to prove. I burn to belong. Passion, when rooted, becomes my strength."

June 9 – The Day of Unfiltered Intimacy

A story of raw presence, emotional transparency, and the kind of closeness that only arrives when you drop the mask and say, "Here I am ~ all of me."

There once was a soul who had learned how to curate closeness.

They shared… but not too much. They loved… but held back their deepest fears. They smiled while bleeding inside.

They believed intimacy meant being accepted ~ so they offered only what they thought others could handle.

Then one evening ~ as the Northern skies blushed in a cascade of orange heat, or the Southern hearth cast flickering shadows across still skin ~ the soul stood before someone they trusted.

Their voice cracked. Their chest tightened. And still… they spoke.

Not in polished words. Not to impress. But to *reveal*.

A truth they'd hidden. A need they feared. A wound they had protected.

And that person didn't leave. They didn't flinch.

They *stayed* ~ not because the soul was perfect, but because they were *real*.

"This," the soul breathed, "is what it feels like to be loved without performance."

Seasonal Awareness:

In the Northern Hemisphere, the heat and energy of summer may tempt you toward performance, confidence, and ease. But unfiltered intimacy asks you to *drop the armor* ~ especially when things feel bright on the outside.

In the Southern Hemisphere, the introspective chill of winter may offer you emotional stillness. Let this season be a portal to say *what's really going on* ~ in the quiet, with warmth, with care.

Wherever you are, today's truth is this: closeness doesn't require polish. It requires presence.

Echoes from Earlier Days:

- On March 5, you spoke a fear you thought no one could hold.
- On May 21, you practiced magnetic honesty.
- On June 3, you stood in loving clarity.

Today brings those practices into unfiltered intimacy ~ the place where nothing is edited, and *everything still belongs*.

Archetype of the Day: *The Barefaced Soul*

This is the self who does not armor up to be loved. Who does not offer only their light. Who trusts that *the whole truth* is what deepens connection ~ not threatens it.

Symbols of the Day:

— A fogged mirror slowly clearing, revealing a soft, unguarded face
— Lepidolite, for nervous system healing, emotional honesty, and gentle release
— The Moon card, emotional truth, shadow exposure, trust beyond clarity
— A dove resting in open hands, safe even in vulnerability

Reflection Prompts:

— What truth have I not yet allowed into the space of my closest relationships?
— Where have I performed emotional safety ~ instead of being honest?
— What would it feel like to say, "This is me, unfiltered" ~ and trust I'll still be held?

Integration Practice: Say the Real Thing

With a partner:

- Create space. Sit without distraction.
- Share one sentence that begins:

"Here's the part of me I've been hiding, even from you…"

- Let it land. Let silence hold it.

Then say:

"Thank you for receiving what is real."

Alone:

- Write a letter to someone you love ~ or to yourself.

Say the thing you've never said out loud. Don't send it. Just witness it.

- Fold it. Hold it to your chest. Say:

"This is me. I am safe to be seen."

Closing Mantra for the Today ~

"I do not perform to be loved. I reveal to be known. Intimacy begins where editing ends."

June 10 – The Day of Sensual Presence

A story of awake attention, sacred stillness, and the kind of intimacy that arises not through touch alone ~ but through total, embodied awareness

There once was a soul who longed to feel more alive in their relationships ~ more present, more desired, more awake.

They believed something was missing. They tried harder. Talked more. Touched more. But the closeness still felt a little… distant.

Then one day ~ as the Northern sun traced golden light across skin, or the Southern chill drew them closer beneath thick covers ~ the soul did something radical:

They *paused*.

They looked. They listened. They breathed ~ with their partner, not over them.

And something shifted.

Every breath was visible. Every eye movement felt like a sentence. Every tiny sound echoed like a sacred bell.

"This," the soul realized, "is sensuality I've never known. Not new sensation ~ but new *presence*."

They didn't need more. They needed to *arrive*.

Seasonal Awareness:

🌑 In the Northern Hemisphere, external stimulation is high ~ color, sound, movement. But true presence asks you to *slow down* within the abundance. Let the sensual world become an anchor, not a distraction.

🌑 In the Southern Hemisphere, the quiet invites intimacy to deepen. Fewer distractions mean the *subtle becomes sacred*. Let every sip of tea, every breath against skin, every shared silence be *felt fully*.

Wherever you are, sensuality is not found in *more*. It's found in *here*.

Echoes from Earlier Days:

— On May 22, you entered into sensory union.

— On May 30, you practiced erotic stillness.

— On June 2, you embraced erotic simplicity.

Today deepens these by reminding you that *nothing is missing* when you are truly present.

Archetype of the Day: *The Present Lover*

This is the self who knows that sensuality begins not with action, but with attention. They feel every inch of the moment. They don't rush to the climax ~ they live inside the rise.

Symbols of the Day:

- A hand slowly brushing through hair, with full presence
- Sandalwood, for grounding sensual awareness and deep breath
- The Ace of Cups, not as emotional flood, but as *pure presence of feeling*
- A cat slowly blinking at the sun, every muscle at ease, every sense alert

Reflection Prompts:

- When was the last time I slowed down enough to feel everything ~ not just touch, but tone, scent, breath, mood?
- What part of my sensual life has been dulled by distraction or routine?
- Can I let presence be the portal to pleasure ~ rather than performance?

Integration Practice: The Five Sense Ceremony

With a partner:

- Sit close. In silence, explore the room or each other through each sense.
  - Sight: Gaze, then close your eyes and describe.
  - Touch: Hands, fabric, skin ~ slow and soft.
  - Sound: Breathe together. Speak one word each.
  - Smell: Share a scent. Let it linger.
  - Taste: Offer something small. Let it melt.

Then whisper:

"I feel you. I am here."

Alone:

- Light incense or diffuse oil. Sip something warm.
- Run your hand over your body ~ not to arouse, but to attune.
- Speak:

"My senses are alive. I am here with myself."

Closing Mantra for the Today ~

"I arrive through attention. I awaken through stillness. My presence is my most sensual gift."

June 11 – The Day of Embodied Honesty

A story of full-body truth, courageous expression, and the intimacy that becomes possible when we don't just speak what's real ~ we live it

There once was a soul who told the truth... but didn't always *live* it.

They said what sounded right. They shared what was safe. They spoke about boundaries ~ and then let them slide. They said they were okay ~ but their body tightened with every "yes" that meant "no."

Until one day ~ as the Northern light filtered through heat-stilled air, or the Southern winds curled cold around their chest ~ their truth caught up with them.

Their throat ached. Their stomach turned. Their heart pounded ~ not from fear, but from *recognition*.

"I've been speaking half-truths," the soul whispered. "Now it's time to embody the whole one."

They stood. They breathed. And for once, they *let their body lead*.

And in that moment, the truth wasn't just said ~ it was *known*. Embodied. Unapologetic. Alive.

Seasonal Awareness:

🌑 In the Northern Hemisphere, heat and movement may tempt you to keep going ~ to perform your truth instead of pause for it. Let June be a checkpoint. Ask: *Does my life reflect what I say I believe?*

🌑 In the Southern Hemisphere, stillness supports integrity. The quiet of winter gives space for recalibration. Let your body tell you what aligns ~ not your mind alone.

Honesty isn't a sentence. It's a stance, a tone, a posture. Your body always knows the real story.

Echoes from Earlier Days:

— On March 14, you touched on radical self-alignment.
— On May 18, you felt the tenderness of showing up with your full emotional self.
— On June 6, you honored devotional desire ~ today, you honor embodied truth.

Archetype of the Day: *The Living Truth*

This self doesn't only speak ~ they act. They align. They express. They don't abandon the body to keep the peace. They are peace ~ because they are whole.

Symbols of the Day:

- A spine standing tall in soft light, unbent by fear
- Blue lace agate, for honest expression, nervous system calm, and embodied voice
- The Queen of Swords, clear, wise, emotionally honest without armoring
- A wolf howling not from rage ~ but from clarity, heard by the trees

Reflection Prompts:

- Where in my life do I say one thing… but feel or live another?
- What truth has my body been holding, waiting for me to acknowledge with action?
- What would it feel like to become the truth I've been trying to explain?

Integration Practice: Body-Aligned Truth-Telling

With a partner:

- Sit facing each other. One person speaks a truth.
- The other watches the speaker's body ~ not just their words.
- Then reflect:

"I saw you come alive when you said…" "I felt truth in your voice when you paused here…"

Alone:

- Stand in front of a mirror. Speak a sentence that scares you ~ out loud.

Watch your face. Feel your breath.

- Then ask:

"Do I believe this?" "Does this feel real in my body?"

- Adjust until your spine, breath, and voice all say yes.

Closing Mantra for the Today ~

"My truth is not just in my words. It lives in my spine, my chest, my breath. I do not just speak it ~ I become it."

June 12 – The Day of Sacred Reconnection

A story of repair, soul remembering, and the healing that becomes possible when you return ~ not to the way things were, but to what is real, right now

There once was a soul who had drifted from someone they loved.

Not through conflict. Not through betrayal. Just… distance.

Little things left unsaid. Moments passed too quickly. A look that once lingered now glanced away.

They told themselves it was fine. Normal. Adult life, routines, exhaustion.

But one afternoon ~ as the Northern trees whispered in summer rhythm, or the Southern air held a stillness too soft to ignore ~ they sat quietly next to this person.

No expectations. No fixing.

Just presence.

And then it happened.

A brush of fingertips. A breath released. A truth shared, quietly:

"I miss us."

Not who they were ~ but what they felt when they were truly present together.

Not a return to old patterns ~ but a reconnection to the *truth beneath them.*

And in that moment, without fireworks or big gestures, love found its way home.

Seasonal Awareness:

◐ In the Northern Hemisphere, warmth brings activity, but often disconnection. Let reconnection come through slowness ~ shared walks, skin-to-skin rest, quiet conversation under sun-dappled trees.

◐ In the Southern Hemisphere, stillness deepens emotional roots. Use this time to reach out, to rebuild trust, to speak softly in candlelight or blanket-covered silence.

Reconnection is not a return to what was ~ it is the brave act of *beginning again from right here.*

Echoes from Earlier Days:

— On April 20, you were invited to reach across emotional distance.

- On May 27, you stepped into mutual awakening ~ growing together again.
- On June 5, you explored wild permission ~ today, that permission includes coming home to each other.

Archetype of the Day: *The Returner*

This is the self who knows that connection isn't permanent ~ it's tended. They are not ashamed to say, *"Let's find our way back."* They move not with guilt, but with grace.

Symbols of the Day:

- Two hands clasping gently over a threshold, neither pulling nor pushing
- Rhodonite, for relationship repair, heart-based courage, and clear love
- The Three of Cups, joyful reconnection, shared vulnerability, chosen family
- A pair of cranes bowing toward one another, elegant and present

Reflection Prompts:

- Who or what have I unintentionally drifted from?
- What reconnection am I craving ~ and what's one small step I can take today?

- Can I allow reconnection to feel gentle ~ not dramatic, but deeply real?

Integration Practice: The Returning Ritual

With a partner:

- Light a candle. Sit facing each other.
- Take turns saying:

"One thing I miss… and one thing I'm still here for."

- Then hold hands in silence ~ no fixing, just presence.

Alone:

- Write a letter to someone (living or not) you wish to reconnect with ~ emotionally, spiritually, energetically.
- Begin:

"I never stopped carrying this connection. I'd like to meet it again."

- Hold it to your heart, then release it ~ or send it, if called.

🕊 Closing Mantra for the Today ~

"I do not return to the past ~ I return to presence. Reconnection begins with truth, softness, and readiness. What is real will rise again, when I meet it with grace."

June 13 – The Day of Vulnerable Fire

A story of courageous tenderness, exposed desire, and the sacred blaze that burns brightest when the heart is unguarded

There once was a soul who had been taught to split their fire from their feelings.

To burn was to be bold. To desire was to be strong. But to cry while wanting, to shake while loving ~ that was weakness.

So they armored up. Loved fiercely, but never gently. Desired fully, but never vulnerably.

Until one night ~ as the Northern stars pulsed in heat-born silence, or the Southern wind curled low against the windows in winter hush ~ the soul let go.

In the middle of touch ~ or perhaps conversation ~ something cracked open. Tears fell not from sadness, but from surrender.

And the one they loved didn't pull away. They pressed their forehead against theirs and said:

"You don't have to choose between passion and softness. You are most beautiful when they meet."

The fire remained ~ but now, it glowed from the inside. No more mask. No more performance. Just vulnerable fire ~ radiant, real, and held.

Seasonal Awareness:

🌕 In the Northern Hemisphere, long, heated days may bring sensual energy ~ but today asks you to slow and soften inside that flame. Let your intensity include tenderness. Let sweat and emotion coexist.

🌑 In the Southern Hemisphere, this is the fire you light *inside* ~ emotional, spiritual, intimate. Let yourself feel deeply, even in the chill. Vulnerability is your warmth now.

Wherever you are, remember: fire doesn't weaken with feeling. It deepens.

Echoes from Earlier Days:

— On May 26, you honored the wisdom of your body's truth.

— On June 7, you surrendered into soulful submission.

— On June 11, you stood in embodied honesty.

Today, these themes converge ~ feeling and flame, raw and radiant.

Archetype of the Day: *The Tender Flame*

This is the self who can cry and burn. Who can say, *"I want you,"* and also *"I'm scared."* Who knows that real passion requires *emotional exposure*, not just heat.

Symbols of the Day:

- A candle burning in a rainstorm ~ still lit, wax melting like tears
- Sunstone, for empowered vulnerability, joy after exposure, and soft passion
- The Knight of Cups reversed, romantic intensity tempered with humility
- A lion walking through a gentle mist, powerful, wet-eyed, unstoppable

Reflection Prompts:

- Have I been separating desire from emotion ~ and what would it look like to reunite them?
- What part of me still believes I have to be strong to be wanted?
- Can I let my tears be sacred ~ not as breakdown, but as truth rising?

Integration Practice: Touch Through Tears

With a partner:

- Begin with eye contact. Hold one another's gaze for 1 minute.
- Speak a truth that holds both vulnerability and desire:

"I want you to see this part of me..."

- Allow silence, emotion, even tears to come.
- Touch only with reverence.

Alone:

- Place a warm hand over your chest.
- Whisper:

"I am safe to want. I am safe to weep. I am radiant in my softness."

- Write:

"The fire I've been hiding is..."

Let the page hold what you haven't yet said aloud.

Closing Mantra for the Today ~

"I am not too much. I am not too soft. My vulnerability is not my wound ~ it is my warmth. I burn, I feel, I stay."

June 14 – The Day of Erotic Equilibrium

A story of balance in desire, mutual consent, and the sacred dance that arises when passion meets presence ~ and both are honored equally

There once was a soul who gave everything in love ~ or nothing at all.

They swung between full surrender and full retreat. Burned brightly, then dimmed into silence. Craved closeness, then panicked when it arrived.

They thought love had to be consuming. That desire meant giving everything ~ or withholding everything.

Then one day ~ as the Northern heat pulsed gently through sunlit sheets, or the Southern dusk curled in like a heavy cloak ~ the soul was met with something unfamiliar.

Balance.

A lover who didn't take too much. A rhythm that asked for nothing more than *presence*. A kiss offered slowly, with no expectation... just invitation.

The soul didn't fall apart. They didn't have to lose themselves. They simply leaned in ~ without disappearing.

"This," they whispered, "is erotic equilibrium. This is what it feels like to burn *and* belong ~ at the same time."

Seasonal Awareness:

🌑 In the Northern Hemisphere, fiery days may tempt overexertion in love and body. Let your sensuality move with balance ~ rest + play, touch + space, yes + pause.

🌑 In the Southern Hemisphere, cooler air may slow the body but deepen connection. Let this be your time to reclaim balance internally ~ between giving and receiving, doing and being.

Desire is not more powerful when it's wild. It's more powerful when it's *mutual*.

Echoes from Earlier Days:

- On May 25, you explored sacred sensation ~ a call to presence over urgency.
- On June 8, you felt the slow burn of grounded passion.
- On June 13, you embraced vulnerable fire.

Today, these lessons culminate ~ passion, but not panic. Presence, but not passivity.

Archetype of the Day: *The Harmonized Lover*

This is the part of you that knows how to stay in yourself while reaching for another. They trust that balance in intimacy does not dilute desire ~ it *deepens* it.

Symbols of the Day:

- A pair of scales gently tilting with flower petals on each side
- Zebra jasper, for balance between opposing energies, sensual harmony, embodied alignment
- The Two of Pentacles, gracefully balancing connection and self
- Two otters floating side-by-side, close but free

Reflection Prompts:

- Do I swing between extremes in desire ~ all in or all out?
- Where am I overgiving or withholding in love or intimacy?
- What does balance in my body and heart feel like ~ and how can I return to it today?

Integration Practice: The Equal Touch Exchange
With a partner:

- Set a timer for 10 minutes each.
- One person gives ~ with full presence. The other receives.
- Then switch. No multitasking. No rushing.

- Afterward, share:

"I felt most connected when…"

Alone:

- Touch your own body with presence ~ hands, arms, neck, belly.
- Ask:

"What does my body want today ~ to be held, moved, expressed, still?"

- Breathe into your answer.

Closing Mantra for the Today ~

"I do not lose myself in desire. I stay present, whole, and awake. My passion flows in balance ~ mutual, sacred, and free."

June 15 – The Day of Inner Union

A story of self-marriage, sacred integration, and the moment you realize that true intimacy begins within ~ where your masculine and feminine meet and make peace

There once was a soul who searched endlessly for "the one."

They craved completion in another. They believed love lived in someone else's arms. They chased union like a finish line.

But every relationship echoed the same imbalance. Something always felt missing ~ until they were finally left alone.

And it was in that solitude ~ as the Northern breeze stirred tall grass into gentle spirals, or the Southern hearth pulsed softly in the still air of winter ~ that the soul saw their reflection.

Not in glass ~ but in silence.

And there they met two parts: The one who gives. The one who receives. The part who acts. And the part who aches.

Not enemies ~ but estranged.

So they lit a candle. Placed one hand over their belly, one on their heart. And whispered vows to themselves:

"I promise to hold you like no one else ever could. To stay. To protect. To soften. I do."

And with that, the union began ~ not with another, but within.

Seasonal Awareness:

🌕 In the Northern Hemisphere, outer life may feel full ~ growth, movement, relationships. But today calls you inward. The union you're seeking *starts in stillness*.

🌑 In the Southern Hemisphere, winter wraps the world in self-reflection. Perfect for inner balancing. Let this be a sacred pause ~ a gentle ceremony of self-acknowledgment and integration.

You are not half a soul. You are your own wholeness, waiting to be recognized.

Echoes from Earlier Days:

— On January 9, you began the path of meeting yourself honestly.

— On March 3, you stepped into divine polarity ~ learning from contrast.

— On May 29, you honored the sacred memory of past love ~ now you root in present wholeness.

Archetype of the Day: *The Inner Beloved*

This is the part of you that no longer looks outward for validation or completion. They live in the meeting place of doing and being, strength and surrender, logic and feeling. They are your home.

Symbols of the Day:

- A ring placed on your own finger, simple, meaningful, yours
- Moonstone + Sunstone, divine feminine and masculine balanced in harmony
- The Lovers card, not external but internal ~ a reflection of soulful wholeness
- A tree with two trunks joined at the root, strong, intertwined, indivisible

Reflection Prompts:

- Where do I still wait for someone else to bring me the love I crave?
- What part of me have I neglected ~ the doer, the feeler, the protector, the nurturer?
- What would it feel like to vow devotion to myself today ~ not just love, but union?

Integration Practice: Self-Marriage Ritual

This can be done solo, or in the presence of a trusted witness.

- Light a candle.
- Place one hand over your belly (masculine), one over your heart (feminine).
- Speak aloud:

"I honor the strength in me. I honor the softness in me. I no longer abandon either. I marry myself in presence, in passion, in peace."

- Optionally, place a symbolic ring, ribbon, or token on your finger or altar.

Let this be the day you choose yourself, fully.

Closing Mantra for the Today ~

"I am not waiting to be completed. I am already whole. My inner union is sacred ~ and from it, all love flows."

June 16 – The Day of Soulful Boundaries

A story of fierce self-protection, tender honesty, and the sacred strength it takes to say: "This is what I need ~ and I still love you."

There once was a soul who feared saying no.

They loved deeply. Gave generously. Bent until they broke ~ calling it care, calling it connection.

But slowly, their inner light began to flicker. They were tired. Resentful. Disconnected from themselves, even as they stayed connected to others.

Then one evening ~ as the Northern world swelled with summer's overstimulation, or the Southern skies hung still and crisp with introspective calm ~ they paused.

Alone.

And in the silence, something rose:

"Love is not unlimited access. Love is the space where I can still find myself."

That night, they wrote a truth they had never said aloud:

- What hurts.
- What's no longer okay.
- What they need ~ not as punishment, but as protection.

And they spoke it. Clearly. Kindly. Firmly.

And something surprising happened.

Love didn't collapse. It *clarified*.

Because soulful boundaries aren't about pushing away ~ they're how we stay close *without losing ourselves*.

Seasonal Awareness:

🌑 In the Northern Hemisphere, today may feel overstimulated ~ sun, sound, energy, connection. Boundaries help you reclaim peace. Create space in your body, your schedule, your relationships.

🌑 In the Southern Hemisphere, the quiet may tempt isolation. Boundaries here are not walls ~ they are invitations for *safe closeness*. Let your "yes" mean yes, your "no" mean rest.

No is not rejection. It's sacred direction ~ toward what nurtures.

Echoes from Earlier Days:

- On February 3, you created your first container of self-protection.
- On May 19, you practiced saying what's sacred ~ even when it might disappoint.
- On June 3, you spoke your loving clarity.

Today, it's time to act on that clarity ~ to draw the circle that keeps your soul intact.

Archetype of the Day: *The Guardian of Self*

This part of you knows that love without boundaries becomes depletion. That saying no is an act of devotion ~ not distance. That every healthy relationship begins with *truthful shape*.

Symbols of the Day:

- A circle of salt around bare feet, protective and grounding
- Black tourmaline, for energetic boundaries, safety, and clarity
- The Seven of Wands, standing firm with conviction and love
- A turtle pulling into its shell, not in fear ~ but in wisdom

Reflection Prompts:

- Where have I been overextending, and what is the cost to my inner peace?
- What boundary have I been afraid to set ~ and why?
- How can I express my limits not with fear or force, but with care and confidence?

Integration Practice: Drawing the Sacred Line

With a partner:

- Begin with appreciation:

"I care deeply for us. And to stay connected, I need to say this…"

- Speak the boundary clearly:

"Here is what I need to feel safe, whole, or present in our connection…"

- Ask:

"Can you meet me here?"

- Then pause. Let it be heard.

Alone:

- Write a list of three boundaries your soul is asking for right now.
- Begin each with:

"For my peace and power, I choose…"

- Speak them aloud. Post them somewhere private as a vow to yourself.

Closing Mantra for the Today ~

"My boundaries are not walls ~ they are invitations. They show others how to love me well. I protect my peace without apology."

June 17 ~ The Day of Erotic Truth

A story of honest desire, raw confession, and the liberation that comes from no longer hiding what you want ~ even from yourself

There once was a soul who kept their desire quiet.

Not because they didn't feel it ~ but because they'd learned to doubt it.

They worried it was too much. Too strange. Too bold. Too soft.

So they watered it down. Laughed it off. Waited for others to guess it ~ but never spoke it aloud.

Then one day ~ as the Northern sky pulsed with restless heat, or the Southern air held heavy breath near firelight ~ the soul reached a threshold.

They couldn't pretend anymore.

Not in intimacy. Not in fantasy. Not in self-denial.

So they sat with a trembling hand and said what they'd never dared say:

"Here's what I want. Here's what I need. And here's what's true for me, even if it's not for you."

And the room didn't collapse.

In fact… it opened.

Because erotic truth, when spoken with courage and consent, is not a threat ~ it's an invitation to be known.

Fully. Finally. Freely.

Seasonal Awareness:

🌑 In the Northern Hemisphere, where desire is ripe and sensation heightened, the temptation may be to act without speaking. Today asks you to *voice* what's rising ~ with honesty and care.

🌑 In the Southern Hemisphere, colder air may suppress or quiet your longing. But erotic truth doesn't disappear ~ it waits to be named. Let this be your day to speak, to write, to *own* what still lives in you.

Truth, when whispered from your depths, is one of the most erotic acts of all.

Echoes from Earlier Days:

- On May 23, you claimed your erotic self-trust.
- On June 6, you honored desire as a sacred offering.
- On June 13, you allowed your vulnerability to burn bright.

Today brings those threads together in one question: Will I speak the truth of my desire ~ without shrinking?

Archetype of the Day: *The Erotic Confessor*

This is the part of you that no longer needs to seduce, hint, or hide. They speak from the heart of the body. They trust that truth is not rejection ~ it's recognition.

Symbols of the Day:

— A lips-parted breath at the edge of confession, tender and brave
— Carnelian + lapis lazuli, for empowered speech and bold sensuality
— The Devil card (reversed) ~ not shame, but freedom from secrecy
— A rose blooming through stone, unapologetic, seen, fully alive

Reflection Prompts:

— What desire have I kept hidden ~ not because it's wrong, but because it's mine?
— Where have I shaped myself around others' comfort, instead of my own longing?
— How would it feel to be seen in what I actually want ~ not just what's easy to receive?

Integration Practice: Truth Without Armor

With a partner:

- Choose a quiet, private moment.
- Say:

"I want to share a desire that lives deep in me…"

- Speak slowly. Name the feeling, the need, the scene, the craving.
- End with:

"You don't have to meet it. But I needed you to know it."

Alone:

- Write an Erotic Truth Letter to yourself.

Begin: *"Here's what I've always wanted to say about my desire…"*

- Read it aloud.
- Whisper:

"You are not too much. You are finally heard."

Closing Mantra for the Today ~

"My desire is not shameful. My truth is not too loud. I speak what I want ~ with grace, with power, with love."

June 18 – The Day of Sacred Mirrors

A story of emotional reflection, intimate resonance, and the deep connection that forms when we see ourselves ~ clearly, bravely ~ in one another

There once was a soul who longed to be understood.

They shared generously. Listened deeply. Loved fully ~ yet still felt unseen in the places that mattered most.

Others appreciated their light... but often missed their depth.

Then one morning ~ as the Northern sun filtered through leaves in golden stillness, or the Southern wind whispered along the spine of winter trees ~ the soul sat beside someone who *really* looked at them.

Not just at their face. Not just at their smile.

But into the *places they thought they had hidden too well.*

No judgment. No rescue. Just presence.

And the soul felt something ancient stir:

"You don't complete me... You *reflect me*. You remind me of who I've always been beneath the noise."

That day, the soul understood ~ True connection isn't built on knowing everything. It's built on being willing to see ~ and be seen ~ without distortion.

Seasonal Awareness:

🌗 In the Northern Hemisphere, light and warmth may encourage social connection. But today, look beyond surface-level contact ~ seek out the *mirror* in your closest relationships.

🌑 In the Southern Hemisphere, quiet days allow room for emotional resonance. Let winter's introspection be the portal through which you ask: *Who reflects the truth of me?* And... *do I let them?*

Sacred mirroring is not about perfection ~ it's about *recognition*.

Echoes from Earlier Days:

— On March 11, you explored your emotional reflection in others.
— On May 24, you practiced deep listening in love.
— On June 9, you revealed yourself through unfiltered intimacy.

Today brings a new layer: allowing yourself to be fully *seen* ~ not for who you've tried to be, but for who you *are* when you stop performing closeness.

Archetype of the Day: *The Soul Mirror*

This is the part of you that holds still enough to be a reflection. They invite emotional resonance by *being real*, not rehearsed. They help others meet themselves, too ~ without fixing, only by *being present*.

Symbols of the Day:

- A still lake reflecting the sky, with no ripples, no distortion
- Sodalite, for deep communication, emotional clarity, and heart-aligned truth
- The Two of Cups, not just romantic union ~ but emotional reciprocity
- A pair of owls perched silently together, aware, awake, unwavering

Reflection Prompts:

- Who mirrors my truth ~ not just my words, but my feelings?
- Where do I fear being seen too clearly ~ and why?
- How might I hold space for someone else's truth, without trying to shape it?

Integration Practice: The Mirror Conversation

With a partner:

— Sit facing one another.

— Take turns completing this sentence:

"When I'm with you, I see the part of myself that…"

— No interruptions. Just listening.

— Afterward, reflect together:

"What do we most clearly reflect back to one another?"

Alone:

— Stand before a mirror. Look into your own eyes.

— Say aloud:

"Today, I meet myself with truth and tenderness. I do not look away."

- Write what you see ~ not appearance, but *essence*.

¶

¶

¶

¶

¶

¶

Closing Mantra for the Today ~

"I reflect what is real. I receive what is true. In seeing others ~ and being seen ~ I come home to myself."

June 19 – The Day of Intimate Integrity

A story of quiet alignment, emotional honesty, and the sacred courage it takes to stay true to yourself ~ even inside your closest connections

There once was a soul who thought love meant compromise.

They softened their voice to avoid conflict. Laughed at jokes that stung. Said yes when their body said no ~ not out of fear, but from *habit*.

They believed intimacy required sacrifice. That connection was about keeping the peace ~ even at the cost of inner clarity.

But one day ~ as the Northern sun climbed into the fullness of summer or the Southern sky stretched wide with introspective hush ~ the soul found themselves mid-conversation, heart pounding.

And instead of shrinking, they said:

"I care about us ~ and I need to stay honest with myself to stay connected with you."

No edge. No blame. Just truth ~ spoken with *love, not defense*.

And something remarkable happened.

They weren't pushed away. They were met. Because the right people don't leave when you're honest ~ they *lean in*.

Seasonal Awareness:

🌑 In the Northern Hemisphere, the energy of the season may lead you outward ~ more activity, more social flow. Let today draw you *inward* ~ to check: Am I acting in alignment with what I *feel?*

🌑 In the Southern Hemisphere, winter is the perfect teacher of boundaries and authenticity. Let the stillness remind you that real connection doesn't require performance ~ only presence.

Integrity in intimacy is not rigidity ~ it's trust. Trust that *you can be loved as you truly are.*

Echoes from Earlier Days:

— On April 9, you reflected on emotional self-respect.

— On May 19, you set boundaries with tenderness.

— On June 11, you embodied your truth fully ~ today, that truth meets relationship.

Archetype of the Day: *The Truth-Keeper in Love*

This is the self who doesn't abandon their inner compass just to stay close. They believe in love that allows for honesty ~ not one that demands silence or shape-shifting.

They speak gently, but firmly. And they know: connection rooted in truth lasts longer than comfort.

Symbols of the Day:

- A single feather standing upright in sand, unwavering and light
- Amazonite, for clear communication, self-trust, and boundary compassion
- The King of Cups, emotionally mature, anchored, and honest in connection
- A wolf resting beside a deer, not devouring, just present ~ balanced, respected

Reflection Prompts:

- Where have I softened myself to avoid discomfort ~ and has it created connection, or confusion?
- What truth is rising in me today, asking to be expressed gently but clearly?
- How do I stay in integrity while staying in love?

Integration Practice: Speak Your Aligned Truth
With a partner:

- Create a quiet moment. Begin with:

"I've been holding back something that matters, because I didn't want to rock the boat..."

- Then say it. Slowly. Without blame, but with clarity.
- Invite the other to respond from listening, not defense.

Alone:

- Write a "Letter of Alignment" to someone (past or present).

Start with: *"Here's what I wish I'd said ~ not to hurt, but to stay true to me…"*

- Burn it, or keep it, depending on what feels most honoring.

Closing Mantra for the Today ~

"I do not trade truth for belonging. I bring all of me ~ gently, clearly, honestly. Real love welcomes what is real in me."

June 20 – The Day of Soulful Reciprocity

A story of mutual giving, emotional balance, and the sacred fulfillment that comes not from giving more ~ but from giving and receiving in harmony

There once was a soul who gave beautifully.

Their presence soothed. Their care ran deep. They held space for others like a shelter in the storm.

But over time, something grew heavy.

They noticed they were always the one reaching out. Always listening, rarely heard. Offering nourishment ~ and quietly starving.

Then one morning ~ as the Northern sun crowned the longest day of light, or the Southern winds carried the hush of winter's midpoint ~ the soul stopped.

Not because they no longer cared. But because they realized:

"This is not connection. This is depletion disguised as devotion."

So they made a choice ~ To receive. To ask. To let the flow move *both ways*.

They reached out ~ not to offer, but to *be held*.

And in that brave reversal, they discovered something unexpected:

True reciprocity does not dilute love ~ It deepens it.

Seasonal Awareness:

🌑 In the Northern Hemisphere, today marks the summer solstice ~ the longest day. With so much light, it's easy to overextend. Let this be a moment to pause and ask: *Where am I giving more than I'm receiving?*

🌑 In the Southern Hemisphere, this is midwinter's still point ~ a sacred time to assess what is nourishing you. Use this reflective pause to ask: *Where can I allow more support, more softness, more shared care?*

The wheel turns, but not alone. We are built for mutual flourishing.

Echoes from Earlier Days:

— On February 7, you learned the power of shared emotional labor.

— On May 28, you honored the simplicity of quiet presence.

— On June 14, you explored balance in intimacy.

Today is a culmination ~ a sacred return to equilibrium in the exchange of love.

Archetype of the Day: *The Giver Who Receives*

This is the self who knows that generosity doesn't mean over-functioning. They are nourished by love *because* they allow it in ~ not just out.

They trust that relationships thrive when built on shared tending.

Symbols of the Day:

- Two hands passing a bowl back and forth, full each time
- Rose quartz + green aventurine, for heart-centered balance and open-hearted receptivity
- The Six of Pentacles, the card of mutual giving, dignity in both offering and receiving
- A circle of migrating birds, taking turns leading and following

Reflection Prompts:

- Where in my life am I giving more than I'm receiving ~ and why?
- What belief makes me feel safer offering than asking?
- How might I open to soulful reciprocity ~ with softness and trust?

Integration Practice: The Shared Exchange

With a partner:

— Sit quietly.

— Take turns completing the sentence:

"Something I've loved giving you is…" "Something I'd love to receive more of from you is…"

— No defense. Just witnessing. Balance begins with honesty.

Alone:

— Write a list:

"Here's what I often give…" "Here's what I rarely allow myself to receive…"

— Choose one act of receiving today: ask for help, allow care, soften your resistance.

Closing Mantra for the Today ~

"I give from fullness. I receive without guilt. In mutual care, I become whole ~ and so do we."

June 21 – The Day of Seasonal Turning

A story of sacred transition, inner rebalancing, and the wisdom that emerges when we honor the natural rhythms of light and dark, growth and stillness, becoming and release

There once was a soul who tried to stay the same.

They clung to routines, identities, ways of being that had once brought safety. They feared change ~ not because they didn't want to grow, but because they didn't know who they'd be on the other side.

But one day ~ as the Northern world paused at the peak of summer's fullness, and the Southern earth exhaled into the hush of the longest night ~ the soul stood still.

Everything around them was shifting. The light. The air. The pull of the season.

And instead of resisting, they asked:

"What part of me is turning, too?"

Not ending. Not beginning. Turning.

The soul realized that just as the Earth tilts with purpose, so do we. That transitions are not breakdowns ~ they are invitations.

To adjust. To listen. To trust the inner movement that mirrors the sky.

Seasonal Awareness:

🌝 In the Northern Hemisphere, today is the Summer Solstice ~ the brightest, longest day. Pause to notice what has grown. Celebrate your expansion. Then ask: *What comes after light? What am I ready to sustain ~ or let gently wane?*

🌚 In the Southern Hemisphere, today is the Winter Solstice ~ the deepest dark. Honor what has been stripped away. Find warmth in reflection. Ask: *What seed is waiting beneath the soil of my stillness? What light will I slowly return to?*

The solstice is not just a seasonal event. It is a soul mirror ~ a sacred turning point.

Echoes from Earlier Days:

— On March 20, you experienced the balance of the equinox.

— On April 1, you began a season of opening.

— On June 1, you honored the wisdom of your body's truth.

Today, those threads weave into a deeper rhythm ~ the reminder that you are cyclical, too.

Archetype of the Day: *The Spiral Walker*

This self trusts the journey isn't linear. They do not resist the curve, the shift, the seasonal pull inward or outward. They walk with the earth's rhythm ~ not against it.

Symbols of the Day:

- A circle split between golden sun and deep blue moon, turning together
- Clear quartz + smoky quartz, for clarity and release, fullness and grounding
- The Wheel of Fortune, ever turning, reminding us that change is the constant
- A tree at twilight, half in light, half in shadow, whole in both

Reflection Prompts:

- Where in my life am I resisting a natural shift ~ and what might happen if I surrendered to the turn?
- What have I outgrown ~ and what is quietly waiting to grow within me?
- How does this solstice mirror something happening in my soul?

Integration Practice: The Turning Point Ritual

Outdoors or near a window, bring two candles ~ one light, one dark.

- Light the bright candle and say:

"I honor what has grown. I bless what has been revealed."

- Light the dark candle and say:

"I trust what is falling away. I welcome the return to stillness."

- Breathe. Place your hands over your heart and belly.
- Whisper:

"I do not rush. I do not resist. I turn, as the seasons do."

Closing Mantra for the Today ~

"I am not behind. I am not lost. I am turning, with purpose, with grace. The light within me knows its own rhythm."

June 22 – The Day of Devotional Presence

A story of sacred attention, embodied stillness, and the quiet kind of love that doesn't perform ~ it simply stays

There once was a soul who thought devotion had to be dramatic.

Grand gestures. Loud declarations. Proof offered in sacrifice and scale.

They gave their time. Their effort. Their everything ~ but often from a place of tension, not trust.

Then one evening ~ as the Northern light softened into golden calm, or the Southern air turned inward with the hush of midwinter dusk ~ the soul found themselves sitting quietly beside someone they loved.

No talking. No touching. Just presence.

They noticed the rise and fall of breath. The rhythm of a heartbeat. The sacred silence that stretched between them ~ not as distance, but as *communion*.

And in that stillness, they understood:

"Devotion is not how much I do. It's how fully I am here."

Not effort, but awareness. Not volume, but *vibrational truth*. To be wholly present is to love completely ~ without agenda.

Seasonal Awareness:

🌑 In the Northern Hemisphere, as summer energy rises, you may be pulled outward. But today calls you *inward*. Let your warmth be less about action ~ and more about attention.

🌑 In the Southern Hemisphere, the stillness of winter invites you to stay. To *be with* what is ~ not to fix, change, or stir. Presence is your devotion now.

Real presence is not passive. It is the deepest act of love we offer.

Echoes from Earlier Days:

— On April 22, you explored the intimacy of quiet connection.

— On May 30, you entered the space of erotic stillness.

— On June 10, you practiced sensual presence.

Today is the *devotional deepening* of that path ~ where stillness becomes *service* to the sacred.

Archetype of the Day: *The Devoted Witness*

This is the self who shows up not to impress, fix, or achieve. They come to *see*. To *be with*. They know that simply staying is an act of reverence.

Symbols of the Day:

- A person seated cross-legged, eyes closed, hand on heart, steady and soft
- Amethyst, for spiritual attunement, meditative calm, and sacred presence
- The Temperance card, quiet balance, embodied trust, soft alignment
- A crane standing still in shallow water, fully alert, fully surrendered

Reflection Prompts:

- Where in my life do I equate love with effort ~ instead of presence?
- Who or what am I being called to be fully present with ~ without needing to fix or change?
- Can I stay ~ really stay ~ with myself, with someone else, with what is, just for today?

Integration Practice: The Presence Offering

With a partner:

- Sit in quiet closeness. No speaking, no phones.
- Place one hand on their heart. Let your breath sync.
- After a few minutes, whisper:

"I'm not here to do anything. I'm here to be with you."

Alone:

- Light a single candle.
- Sit or lie down, hand on your chest.
- For 5 minutes, simply breathe and say:

"I am here. I am not leaving. I am enough in my presence."

Closing Mantra for the Today ~

"My love is not measured by effort ~ but by presence. I give my attention as my offering. I stay ~ because presence is sacred."

June 23 – The Day of Heart-Safe Expression

A story of gentle truth-telling, emotional safety, and the sacred courage it takes to speak from the heart ~ without fear of being misunderstood

There once was a soul who silenced their truth to keep the peace.

They swallowed emotion. Softened their words. Smiled when their voice ached to say more.

They didn't lie ~ but they *withheld*. Not to deceive, but to protect what felt too tender to risk.

Then one afternoon ~ as the Northern air shimmered in summer's golden hum, or the Southern wind curled gently around the edges of an early night ~ the soul stood on the edge of conversation.

Their chest fluttered. Their throat tightened. Their heart beat like a drum not of warning, but of invitation.

So they took a breath and said it ~ Not harshly, not perfectly, but with care:

"I want to share something... and I hope it can be received gently."

And to their surprise, the world didn't collapse.

In fact, something softened. Something opened. Because expression, when rooted in safety, doesn't rupture ~ it *restores*.

Seasonal Awareness:

🌑 In the Northern Hemisphere, summer brings vibrant connection ~ but also emotional intensity. Let this day be a cooling pause: a space to speak without heat, and be heard without defense.

🌑 In the Southern Hemisphere, midwinter stillness creates a sacred container for truth. Let yourself open slowly. Speak with warmth. Invite emotional honesty without rushing it.

Safe expression doesn't need to shout. It simply needs to be *allowed*.

Echoes from Earlier Days:

— On May 6, you explored the connection between breath and truth.

— On June 11, you practiced embodied honesty.

— On June 19, you held your truth gently inside relationship.

Today expands that honesty into expression ~ with care, with heart, with reverent tone.

Archetype of the Day: *The Heart Speaker*

This self does not weaponize truth ~ they *weave* it. They trust that their voice matters, but they also know that how we speak is part of what makes love safe.

Symbols of the Day:

- A candle flickering as words are spoken into the air, calm and clear
- Aquamarine, for heart-aligned communication, courage, and grace
- The Page of Cups, emotional openness, gentle vulnerability, heart-in-hand
- A fawn stepping from the trees, curious, cautious, willing to be seen

Reflection Prompts:

- What truth have I been waiting to say ~ and what fear has kept it hidden?
- How can I speak today not from defense, but from devotion?
- What makes me feel safe to share ~ and how can I offer that safety to others, too?

Integration Practice: Voice from the Heart

With a partner:

- Begin with presence. Sit close, eyes soft.
- Say aloud:

"I want to share something that matters to me. Please listen with love."

- Speak your truth, then thank them for receiving.
- Switch roles. Let the space hold *both truths*.

Alone:

- Place one hand on your throat, one on your heart.
- Speak aloud a sentence you've never said before.

Even if it's just: *"I want to be more seen."*

- Breathe. Receive your own words as sacred.

Closing Mantra for the Today ~

"My voice is an offering. I speak with care. I listen with love. In safety, truth becomes a bridge ~ not a blade."

June 24 – The Day of Emotional Sanctuary

A story of inner refuge, safe connection, and the sacred art of creating a space ~ within and around you ~ where emotions can land, soften, and be held

There once was a soul who never felt safe to fall apart.

They were the strong one. The dependable one. The one others leaned on ~ even when they were quietly crumbling.

They built walls not to keep love out, but to keep breakdown in. Because somewhere along the way, they learned:

"There is no room for my softness."

But one day ~ as the Northern trees hummed with summer fullness, or the Southern frost clung to windows like whispered invitation ~ the soul sat in stillness.

And something in them finally asked:

"Where can I go to fall open? Where is my emotional sanctuary?"

It wasn't a place. It wasn't a person. It was a way of *being* ~ of choosing softness in a world that rushes past emotion.

So they lit a candle. Held a pillow close. And whispered to themselves what they'd longed to hear:

"You don't have to hold it all. You're allowed to be held."

Seasonal Awareness:

🌗 In the Northern Hemisphere, outward movement is at its peak ~ but today asks for pause. Where is your quiet corner? Your moment of inner shade? Even in summer, you need sanctuary.

🌘 In the Southern Hemisphere, winter offers the invitation naturally. Let your home, your breath, your body become a place where feelings don't have to be fixed ~ only felt.

You do not need to perform your strength. You need to be *received*.

Echoes from Earlier Days:

— On January 17, you created space for emotional release.

— On April 30, you honored the soul's need for shelter.

— On June 22, you practiced devotional presence ~ today, you offer that presence to your own heart.

Archetype of the Day: *The Emotional Guardian*

This self creates space ~ not solutions. They hold emotion like a sacred guest. They understand that comfort isn't always about fixing ~ sometimes, it's about *witnessing without rush*.

Symbols of the Day:

- A soft nest of blankets lit by golden window light, untouched and waiting
- Lepidolite + rose quartz, for emotional grounding, heart-healing, and softness
- The Four of Swords, retreat, rest, sacred emotional recuperation
- A mother bear curled around her cub, not in protection ~ but in peace

Reflection Prompts:

- Where in my life do I feel emotionally safe ~ and where do I still armor up?
- What would it mean to become my own sanctuary ~ not in isolation, but in tenderness?
- How can I offer sanctuary to someone else, not by solving ~ but by simply being present?

Integration Practice: Create a Sanctuary Moment
With a partner:

- Sit close without expectation. One speaks; the other *holds space*.
- Say:

"You don't have to fix this. I just need somewhere to land."

— Trade roles. Let silence be your shared container.

Alone:

- Choose a space today that feels nurturing ~ a corner, a chair, a window.
- Light a candle. Wrap yourself in warmth.
- Say aloud:

"I am my own sanctuary. I welcome my feelings home."

Closing Mantra for the Today ~

"I offer myself the space to feel. I do not rush what is sacred. In rest, in quiet, in kindness ~ I come home to myself."

June 25 – The Day of Tender Courage

A story of quiet bravery, emotional softness, and the strength that rises not with armor ~ but with open hands, open heart, and a steady voice that quivers but speaks anyway

There once was a soul who thought courage meant being loud.

Bold moves. Big decisions. No fear, no falter.

They believed bravery was something others could see ~ something that looked impressive from the outside.

But then, on a simple day ~ as the Northern winds stilled under soft light, or the Southern frost kissed the glass like a silent benediction ~ the soul did something very small:

They said what was true. They asked for what they needed. They cried, and didn't apologize.

No shouting. No scene. Just a moment of full-hearted presence ~ without flinching.

And it changed everything.

Because courage is not always a roar. Sometimes, it's a whisper that says:

"I will stay soft… and still show up."

Seasonal Awareness:

🌑 In the Northern Hemisphere, long days may fill your calendar and drain your nervous system. Tenderness is your brave act today.

Choose slowness.

Choose presence.

Choose what is real, even when it's not loud.

🌘 In the Southern Hemisphere, winter wraps you inward. It may feel easier to retreat than to express. But courage doesn't mean exposure ~ it means truth, even in quiet.

Let your voice tremble.

Let your heart lead.

Strength does not mean hardening. It means loving ~ *even when it's scary*.

Echoes from Earlier Days:

— On February 20, you took your first risk toward emotional honesty.
— On April 12, you stood inside your heart's request.
— On June 13, you embraced vulnerable fire ~ today, you hold that fire with grace.

Archetype of the Day: *The Brave Soft-Heart*

This is the self who does not hide their tenderness to be safe. They trust their emotions as part of their wisdom. They do not pretend ~ they *persist* through authenticity.

They lead with heart ~ and let that be enough.

Symbols of the Day:

- A feather pressed gently into damp earth, light but unbroken
- Rhodochrosite, for emotional courage, gentle truth, and soft strength
- The Strength card (feminine aspect) ~ inner steadiness, not domination
- A swan gliding across still water, calm, alert, quietly powerful

Reflection Prompts:

- Where have I mistaken strength for silence ~ and what would true courage look like today?
- What do I long to say, ask, or reveal ~ that would feel brave simply to name?
- Can I meet my emotions with reverence, instead of resistance?

Integration Practice: Small Acts of Tender Bravery

With a partner:

— Share one sentence that begins:

"It's hard for me to say this, but I want to…"

— Pause. Let the silence hold the truth.
— The other replies:

"Thank you for your courage. I see you."

Alone:

— Write a letter to your younger self, who learned to hide feelings to survive.

End with: *"You were always brave. You still are."*

— Fold the letter and place it under your pillow as a sacred vow.

Closing Mantra for the Today ~

"I lead with love, not fear. My softness is not weakness ~ it is my truth. I walk in courage, even when my voice trembles."

June 26 – The Day of Shared Healing

A story of mutual restoration, compassionate witnessing, and the sacred power that emerges when we choose to heal not alone ~ but alongside one another

There once was a soul who believed healing was a solo path.

They carried their pain quietly. Journaled in silence. Wept behind closed doors. They feared their wounds were too much ~ or that healing would burden someone else.

But one afternoon ~ as the Northern sun shimmered through branches thick with bloom, or the Southern sky dimmed in a cocoon of soft gray ~ they sat with someone and, for the first time, *didn't hide the ache.*

They spoke. Not for advice. Not for pity.

But because they needed to be heard.

And in return, the other offered their own story ~ not to compare, but to *join*.

Tears met tears. Hands rested beside one another. Two journeys, side by side ~ no pressure, just presence.

"I don't need to fix you," one said. "I just want to walk with you."

And that was healing, too.

Seasonal Awareness:

🌑 In the Northern Hemisphere, this is a season of outward celebration ~ but even in light, we carry shadows. Today asks: *Where do I need shared space to heal beneath the surface of summer?*

🌑 In the Southern Hemisphere, introspective stillness is everywhere. But isolation need not be your only path. Let someone into your quiet today. Healing is amplified in presence ~ *not diminished by it.*

Healing is not always an inner solo flame. Sometimes, it's two lights held close ~ brightening one another.

Echoes from Earlier Days:

— On March 22, you honored ancestral and emotional healing.
— On May 9, you began tending old wounds with new love.
— On June 12, you made space for sacred reconnection ~ now, that reconnection becomes restoration.

Archetype of the Day: *The Healing Companion*

This self does not try to fix. They walk beside. They know that listening is its own medicine ~ and that healing ripples outward when it's shared with care, not shame.

Symbols of the Day:

- Two candles lit from the same flame, burning steadily side by side
- Malachite, for heart-centered healing, grief support, and deep compassion
- The Three of Pentacles, community collaboration, shared effort, sacred building
- A wound wrapped in soft linen, not hidden ~ but *tended*

Reflection Prompts:

- What part of my healing have I kept private out of fear ~ and who might hold it with care?
- How can I be a witness to someone else's healing today ~ not as a savior, but as support?
- Where have I underestimated the power of shared presence in my journey?

Integration Practice: The Healing Circle

With a partner or small group:

- Sit in a circle or across from one another.
- Each person completes the sentence:

"One part of me that's healing is…"

- No responses. Just deep listening.
- Close with:

"May we each be restored in our time, in our way."

Alone:

- Write the phrase:

"I am not alone in this. Others are healing with me."

- Light a candle. Place both hands on your heart.
- Speak:

"I honor my path. I welcome companionship. I allow shared light to help me rise."

¶
¶
¶

Closing Mantra for the Today ~

"I do not need to carry it all alone. In love, in presence, in shared truth ~ I heal. Together, we mend. Together, we rise."

June 27 – The Day of Sensory Awakening

A story of embodied awareness, soulful aliveness, and the sacred experience of coming home to the world through your five senses ~ and beyond

There once was a soul who lived mostly in their mind.

They planned. They analyzed. They moved through each day like a to-do list with legs.

But something always felt distant ~ like the world was slightly out of reach.

Then one morning ~ as the Northern breeze carried jasmine and sunlight through the open air, or the Southern chill filled the lungs with crisp, clear breath ~ the soul stopped mid-step.

They noticed the warmth of a cup in their hand. The grain of the wood beneath their fingers. The way the light kissed the edge of the room.

And in that pause, they *landed* ~ fully, finally, in their body.

A tear came. Not from sadness, but from presence.

"This," they whispered, "is what I've been missing ~ not meaning, but *sensation*. I am awake. I am here."

From that moment, the soul no longer rushed past life. They touched. Tasted. Breathed. They lived from the skin *inward*.

Seasonal Awareness:

🌗 In the Northern Hemisphere, your senses are vibrant. Use today to *savor* rather than consume. Let sensation be your meditation. Feel the breeze, sip the fruit, trace your fingertips along the moment.

🌑 In the Southern Hemisphere, you may feel dulled by cold or routine. But within stillness lies subtlety. Let yourself notice ~ the softness of blankets, the crackle of fire, the flavor of warm tea. *Sensation will find you, if you let it in.*

The body is not a distraction from the sacred. It is how the sacred *finds you*.

Echoes from Earlier Days:

— On May 22, you explored sensual union as a form of reverence.

— On June 4, you grounded desire through slowness and embodiment.

— On June 10, you learned presence as a portal to deeper intimacy.

Today, those threads are woven together ~ into a felt experience of soul through skin.

Archetype of the Day: *The Awakened Body*

This is the self who does not rush. They do not numb or override. They let the moment enter through every pore ~ and know that feeling is the path to remembering.

Symbols of the Day:

- A bowl of ripe fruit glistening in sunlight, untouched and sacred
- Red jasper + honey calcite, for root and solar awakening, grounding through sensation
- The Ace of Pentacles, new beginnings through embodiment and the physical realm
- A butterfly resting on bare skin, felt before it's seen

Reflection Prompts:

- Which of my senses have I been ignoring or rushing past ~ and why?
- What does it feel like when I slow down enough to truly notice touch, taste, scent, sound, and sight?
- Can I let today's sensations be my spiritual practice ~ my anchor, my aliveness?

Integration Practice: The Five-Sense Awakening

Alone or with a partner, slowly explore:

- Touch – Run your fingers over fabric, skin, or natural textures. Feel without labeling.
- Taste – Eat something slowly. Let it melt on your tongue.
- Scent – Inhale something familiar. Let memory rise.
- Sight – Choose one object and observe it with reverence.
- Sound – Close your eyes and listen for the quietest thing you can hear.

Afterward, whisper:

"I am here. I feel. I am alive in every sense."

Closing Mantra for the Today ~

"I return to my senses. My body is a prayer ~ each breath, each touch, each taste. I awaken through awareness, and come home to now."

June 28 – The Day of Inner Nourishment

A story of deep replenishment, sacred self-care, and the soulful truth that sustenance begins from within ~ long before it's offered by the world

There once was a soul who fed everyone else first.

They poured love. Gave energy. Stayed up late to soothe others, rose early to meet demands.

They were admired. Appreciated. But secretly ~ depleted.

Their own hunger went unnoticed, even to themselves.

Until one quiet morning ~ as the Northern sun filtered softly through fruit-heavy branches, or the Southern wind wrapped their body in a blanket of cold silence ~ they paused at the table.

Nothing fancy. Just warm tea. A simple bowl of food.

And before offering a thing to the world, they whispered:

"Today, I nourish me first."

Not selfishly. But soulfully.

They ate slowly. Breathed deeply. Touched their own arm with care.

And in that sacred act of tending ~ their spirit began to bloom again.

Because you can only pour from a cup that's full. And sometimes, the most generous thing you can do… is feed your own soul.

Seasonal Awareness:

◐ In the Northern Hemisphere, abundance is all around ~ fruit, sun, community. But without slowing down, even bounty can become burnout. Let today be your reminder: *receive the nourishment you so freely give.*

◑ In the Southern Hemisphere, nourishment may require effort. In the cold, it's easy to retreat or neglect your own care. Today calls you inward ~ to cook something warm, to hold your own hands, to speak to your body gently.

You are not a machine. You are a garden ~ and gardens must be fed.

Echoes from Earlier Days:

— On February 10, you honored the art of sacred rest.

— On May 2, you explored sensual replenishment.

— On June 20, you found balance in soulful reciprocity.

Today, you meet those lessons again ~ not in theory, but in bodily devotion.

Archetype of the Day: *The Inner Provider*

This is the self who tends the body, not just the mission. Who asks, *"What do I need?"* Who fills their cup without apology ~ knowing that love flows stronger from a nourished soul.

Symbols of the Day:

- A wooden bowl filled with berries and cream, glistening in early light
- Moonstone + citrine, for emotional replenishment and joy-filled restoration
- The Nine of Pentacles, self-nourishment, ease, independence with grace
- A deer drinking at the edge of a quiet stream, undisturbed, steady

Reflection Prompts:

- What have I been feeding others that I've withheld from myself?
- Where in my body, spirit, or mind do I feel undernourished today?
- What small act of care would feel most honest and needed right now?

Integration Practice: The Sacred Meal for One

Prepare or gather something nourishing ~ simple or special.

- Set it down in front of you with intention.
- Light a candle or take a breath of gratitude.
- Say aloud:

"This is for me. I deserve to be fed, in every way."

Eat slowly. No phone. No guilt. Just reverence.

If with a partner:

- Feed each other small bites.
- Look into each other's eyes and ask:

"Are you feeling nourished ~ emotionally, physically, spiritually?"

- Listen. Then respond with love.

Closing Mantra for the Today ~

"I nourish myself without shame. I am worthy of care, of sweetness, of enough. From fullness, I rise ~ soft, steady, whole."

June 29 ~ The Day of Quiet Devotion

A story of sacred rhythm, gentle loyalty, and the soft, consistent acts of care that deepen our lives ~ not with grand gestures, but with presence that never leaves

There once was a soul who thought devotion had to look impressive.

They imagined temple bells. Vows spoken beneath moonlight. Big, visible acts of love and meaning.

But those moments were rare.

And in the spaces between, they often felt lost ~ disconnected from spirit, from love, from purpose.

Then one morning ~ as the Northern sun rose with understated warmth, or the Southern mist wrapped the hills in reverent silence ~ the soul stirred their tea.

Lit a candle. Fed their body. Said a simple thank you to the day.

And something *opened*.

A quiet voice inside whispered:

"This is devotion, too."

Not performance. Not perfection. But presence ~ repeated, rooted, real.

Devotion, they realized, isn't something you show off. It's something you live, again and again, in the small, sacred moments.

Seasonal Awareness:

🌑 In the Northern Hemisphere, long days and high energy may distract from inward presence. Today reminds you: devotion doesn't demand effort ~ it asks only for your awareness.

🌑 In the Southern Hemisphere, darkness lingers. Let this be a day to find your personal rhythm ~ through ritual, tea, prayer, journaling, touch. Even in stillness, your consistency is holy.

The sacred is not always loud. Sometimes it sounds like *your own breath*, returning.

Echoes from Earlier Days:

— On January 5, you planted seeds of intentional rhythm.

— On April 6, you learned to bow to the ordinary as sacred.

— On June 22, you honored devotional presence ~ today, you make it a practice.

Archetype of the Day: *The Gentle Keeper*

This is the self who shows up without spectacle. They stir the pot, light the candle, speak the blessing ~ not for applause, but for alignment.

They know that the most powerful change comes from the smallest, repeated reverence.

Symbols of the Day:

- A cup of tea resting beside a worn book, steam curling in the light
- Smoky quartz + white agate, for grounding, consistency, and sacred simplicity
- The Hierophant (softened) ~ ritual, spiritual lineage, devotion to the daily
- A pair of hands weaving the same thread day after day, never rushing

Reflection Prompts:

- What have I mistaken as "not enough" because it was quiet or simple?
- Where in my life am I already devoted ~ and how can I honor that more deeply?
- What daily ritual would bring me closer to myself, to spirit, to the life I love?

Integration Practice: A Devotion of Your Own

Choose something small you can return to every day ~ Lighting a candle. Touching your heart. Writing one sentence of gratitude.

Say aloud:

"This is my devotion. This is my thread. I return not to impress ~ but to remember."

If with a partner:

- Take turns naming one quiet way you've felt loved lately.
- Then offer a gesture of devotion ~ a touch, a word, a shared silence ~ no performance, only presence.

Closing Mantra for the Today ~

"My life is a sacred rhythm. I return to what matters, again and again. In devotion, I am grounded. In simplicity, I am whole."

June 30 – The Day of Inner Celebration

A story of quiet joy, personal acknowledgment, and the sacred truth that you do not need a crowd to celebrate your growth ~ only the courage to witness yourself fully

There once was a soul who waited for permission to celebrate.

They thought joy required a reason. A milestone. An audience.

They downplayed their wins. Minimized their growth. Moved the goalposts again and again.

Until one morning ~ as the Northern skies burst with late-summer brightness, or the Southern hearth crackled with midwinter warmth ~ the soul looked back.

At where they had been. At who they had become. At what they had endured ~ and how they kept showing up.

And in the stillness, without applause or praise, they whispered:

"I am proud of me."

They lit a candle ~ not for someone else, but for themselves. They danced, quietly. They smiled without needing a witness.

Because they had learned: Celebration is not something given to you. It's something you grant yourself.

Seasonal Awareness:

🌕 In the Northern Hemisphere, June closes in full bloom. Before rushing into July, take a pause. Reflect. Celebrate *not just the harvest ~ but the inner work that led to it.*

🌑 In the Southern Hemisphere, winter nears its midpoint. Even in stillness, joy lives. Let this be a celebration of *resilience, reflection, and soulful presence.*

You don't need streamers to recognize your evolution. You just need *a moment of truth.*

Echoes from Earlier Days:

— On March 18, you gave yourself credit for emotional effort.
— On May 1, you opened to joy without guilt.
— On June 15, you honored your inner union ~ today, you *celebrate it.*

Archetype of the Day: *The Self-Honorer*

This is the self who throws a party for their own courage. Who clinks glasses with their reflection. Who no longer waits to be validated ~ because they know their journey is worthy, with or without witnesses.

Symbols of the Day:

- A single cupcake with a candle, lit in the quiet of morning
- Sunstone + pink tourmaline, for joy, self-love, and emotional warmth
- The Nine of Cups, satisfaction, inner fulfillment, celebration without needing more
- A bird singing alone in a wide field, unafraid, fully alive

Reflection Prompts:

- What can I celebrate today ~ not because it's perfect, but because it's honest?
- What version of me has grown that I haven't yet acknowledged?
- What would it feel like to throw a small ceremony for my own becoming?

Integration Practice: Your Celebration, Your Way
Alone:

- Write yourself a love letter.

Begin: *"I see how far you've come. I celebrate you for…"*

- Light a candle. Play music. Toast yourself ~ even if it's with tea.
- Smile in the mirror and say:

"You did that. You're still here. And I'm so proud."

With a partner or friend:

- Share one meaningful shift from this month.
- Let the other reflect it back to you, no fixing, just honoring.
- Close with:

"Let's celebrate the soul work, not just the success."

Closing Mantra for the Today ~

"I do not wait for a reason to celebrate. I am reason enough. In my journey, my joy, my becoming ~ I honor myself today."

June Reflection

The Body Remembers

A Soft Return to Inner Truth. This month invited you into your body ~ not just as a vessel, but as a voice.

You may have found joy in touch, fear in slowness, tenderness in truth, and strength in stillness.

June wasn't about speed ~ it was about subtle courage.

- You learned to stay present, to be vulnerable, to move honestly.
- You listened to your longing ~ not just in words, but in sensation.

This month, the lessons were not always loud. They were felt. And now, as the door closes on June, you're asked:

What has your body learned that your mind is only beginning to understand?

📖 Journal Reflections

Choose 1–3 questions that speak most to your experience:

- What moment this month brought you most into your body ~ and what did it teach you?
- How has your relationship to desire, touch, rest, or expression shifted since June 1?
- Where did you show up with gentle courage ~ even if no one else saw it?
- What's one boundary, one ritual, or one truth you now trust more deeply?
- How has your view of intimacy ~ with self or others ~ changed this month?
- What have you stopped hiding… and what is now safe to feel?

Bonus prompt: *If your soul wrote a thank-you note to your body today, what would it say?*

Sacred Integration Practice: Trace the Journey

Take a quiet hour this week to revisit key entries:

- Re-read June 4 – The Day of Rooted Sensuality → What felt unsafe to express then? What feels possible now?
- Revisit June 13 – The Day of Vulnerable Fire → How do you now carry fire and feeling in balance?

- Reflect on June 29 – The Day of Quiet Devotion →
  What daily act of care or presence has stayed with you?

Use colored pens or sticky notes to mark key insights. Highlight words that land in your body. Trust what resonates.

⊚ Practical Embodiment Strategies

(For Northern & Southern Hemispheres)

☼ Northern Hemisphere (Mid–Late Summer)

- Take your journal outside. Let the sun touch your skin.
- Move barefoot for at least 5 minutes each day this week ~ grass, earth, tile, whatever is real.
- Let your next "yes" come from the body first ~ not the brain.
- Eat something ripe and sweet. Let it remind you of your own ripeness.

❄ Southern Hemisphere (Midwinter)

- Light a candle each morning before speaking or scrolling.
- Wrap yourself in intentional layers ~ your clothes become part of your care.

- Reclaim slow sensuality: warm baths, scented oils, thick soup.
- Sit by a window with tea. Ask, *What does my body need to restore today?*

Closing Mantra for the Month

"My body is my companion, my compass, my truth. I listen without rushing. I love without hiding. I grow through presence, one breath at a time."

Notes

Your Journey Deepens...

Well done!

You've journeyed through Origins of Opening ~ not as a sprint, but as a sacred unfolding.

For 91 days, you've softened into presence, trusted your truth, and allowed your inner world to gently emerge.

- You've listened to your body's wisdom.
- You've dared to speak your longings.
- You've opened ~ even when it felt unfamiliar.

But

But now... something else is calling, isn't it?

A pull below the surface.

A shadow at the edge of the light.

A quiet voice asking,

"What have I yet to face, feel, or reclaim?"

That's where *Volume 3 ~ Unveiling the Unknown* begins.

The next 92 days are not about clarity ~ they are about courage. They are about shadow work, sacred honesty, and meeting the parts of yourself you've outgrown, forgotten, or feared.

- If Volume 1 taught you to arrive...
- If Volume 2 showed you how to open.

Volume 3 will invite you to see

To see what you've hidden.

To see what you've projected.

To see what's possible when nothing is denied ~ only embraced. You are not falling apart. You are falling deeper into truth.

So take one more breath. Light a candle. And walk bravely into the next passage of your soul's spiral.

Not to fix. Not to perfect.

But to *unveil* what's already waiting in the dark ~ whole, worthy, and wildly alive.

www.ingramcontent.com/pod-product-compliance
Lightning Source LLC
LaVergne TN
LVHW020925090426
835512LV00020B/3204